AmeriCorps

Serve your country and pay for college

CONWAY GREENE  PUBLISHING COMPANY

ISBN 1-884669-12-3

Printed in USA

For information please call Conway Greene Co.
216/721-0077 or toll free at 800/977-2665
Or Fax: 216/721-8256

Other books from Conway Greene:

Athletic Scholarships: A Complete Guide
ISBN: 1-884669-05-0

Art & Design Scholarships: A Complete Guide
ISBN: 1-884669-06-9

Music, Dance & Theater Scholarships: A Complete Guide
ISBN: 1-884669-07-7

School-to-Work Programs: A State-by-State Guide
ISBN: 1-884669-04-2

Sports, Everyone! Recreation and Sports for the Physically Challenged of All Ages
ISBN: 1-884669-10-7

JOBS: Planning Your Career Path Through America's Leading Industries
ISBN: 1-884669-11-5

INTRODUCTION

On September 21, 1993, President Clinton signed into law the National Community Service Trust Act, popularly known as "National Service."

National Service addresses two policy issues: the high cost of education and a renewal of commitment to community service. The centerpiece of National Service is the opportunity for students to perform community service in approved programs and earn education awards in return for this service. As President Clinton stated on May 5, 1993, in his message to Congress which accompanied the proposed act:

> Higher education is fundamental to the American Dream, but complex procedures and inflexible repayment plans have created serious problems for many students with education loans to pay back. Defaults are too high today—and taxpayers are left to foot the bill. Americans are yearning to reaffirm an American community that transcends race, region, or religion—and to tackle the problems that threaten our shared future.

Already National Service—also called AmeriCorps has put thousands of young workers into communities. They are earning a living stipend as well as accruing educational awards which can be used for future education or to pay back student loans. Just as important, they are gaining valuable work experience even as they contribute to the health of their communities. As the profiles which follow show, AmeriCorps participants are also able to get a fix on their own futures these months in the field.

You should use this directory to locate and contact programs that interest you. You should expect that programs will change over the course of a year. You may want to contact the state commission in your own state, or a state where you would like to work, as well as the National AmeriCorps office.

Please write to us at Conway Greene about your AmeriCorps experiences. We would be pleased to include your profile in the next edition of this book. Send correspondence to Conway Greene Publishing Company, 11000 Cedar Avenue, Cleveland, OH 44106. Or call toll free at 800/977-2665.

The Publisher

National Service Facts and How to Get Involved

What Is AmeriCorps?

AmeriCorps is the new national service initiative signed into law by President Clinton to create a domestic Peace Corps. It was launched in September 1994 at a White House ceremony and at ceremonies around the country.

- ELIGIBILITY

You must be 17 years or older (16 for some youth programs); a U.S. citizen, national, or legal resident; and, in most cases, a high school graduate or equivalent. You are accepted to a particular position in a National Service program.

- KINDS OF SERVICE

The service is community-based and results-oriented. There are 4 key areas (or "priorities"): Education; Public Safety; Human Needs; and Environment.

- LIVING ALLOWANCE AND EDUCATIONAL AWARD

In exchange for 1 or 2 years of service, you will receive a living allowance averaging $7,500/year; health care; child care; and an educational award of $4,725/year to finance high education or to pay back your student loans. You may be eligible to serve part-time and receive an education award of $2,362. To receive the educational award you must be enrolled in an institution of higher learning or have a waiver. Normally the award must be used within seven years from the completion of the service.

- WHAT IS FULL-TIME SERVICE?

Full-time service is a minimum of 1700 hours over 9 months–1 year.

- WHAT IS PART-TIME SERVICE?

Depending on the local program you could serve part-time for a minimum of 900 hours over 2–3 years.

- WHEN WOULD YOU SERVE?

You could serve after high school; in some cases while working towards your GED; during or after college, vocational school, or graduate school.

- WHERE WOULD YOU SERVE?

You could serve in your own community or anywhere in the country. National Service is a national initiative.

- WHAT ARE THE NATIONAL SERVICE PROGRAMS?

There are two types:

1/"National direct" (also called the "National Service Network") programs either run by federal agencies (such as the Department of Veterans Affairs and HUD) or by national organizations (such as Habitat for Humanity).

2/"Local" or "State" programs, run by service organizations and institutions within each state.

Both types of programs are administered at the local level. In this *Guide*, you will find all contact information, whether the program is national or local/state in each state's listing behind Tab C. An index to the programs by type of program (e.g., AIDS/HIV counseling; conflict resolution and management; watershed restoration) may be found behind Tab D of this *Guide*.

- ARE THERE OTHER AMERICORPS PROGRAMS IN ADDITION TO NATIONAL SERVICE?

Yes. VISTA and National Civilian Community Corps (CCC) are now under the AmeriCorps umbrella. You can apply for either of these programs directly to the Corporation for National Service. Contact AmeriCorps directly to request VISTA or CCC applications.

How to Apply for a
National Service Position

- HOW TO APPLY

There are many ways to contact AmeriCorps and related programs. You may use any of the following contacting methods. As you will see, most of the recruiting is done at the local program level, so eventually you will have to be in touch with the service program directly.

1. Call the AmeriCorps 800 number: 1-800-94-ACORPS and request the AmeriCorps National Referral Form to apply.

2. Call the Commission in your state. They are the AmeriCorps offices at the state level. Their phone and fax numbers, contact persons, and addresses are found in this book.

3. If you live in one state and want to perform national service in another state, call the Commission in the other state. You will find all contact information you need in this book. Do not hesitate to contact out-of-state Commissions and programs. AmeriCorps' goal is to place at least 25% of all participants out of their home states in order to create a truly national program.

4. If you are ready to contact a program directly, you will find the complete list of approved state and national direct programs in his book, with all available contact and program information.

- WHO RECRUITS?

75% of all recruiting is done at the local program level according to their timetable and criteria within the parameters of the AmeriCorps program. Some programs have applications while others request cover letters and resumes. You will need to check with each program individually for application information.

25% of the recruitment is done by AmeriCorps. The AmeriCorps National Referral Form is reprinted here so you can see the questions it contains. You can easily request one from AmeriCorps using the phone numbers above. When you send back the form, you will automatically become a member of the AmeriCorps National Service Network Data Base that will be used to supplement local AmeriCorps Members with national recruits.

- IS NATIONAL SERVICE COMPETITIVE?

Yes. The President announced at the launch on September 12, 1994, that there were over 100,000 inquiries for the 20,000 positions slated for year 1.

- IS IT TOO LATE TO APPLY?

No. Many programs still have slots open and many will be accepting more participants.

A copy of the AmeriCorps Referral Form follows on pages *xi-xii*.

The Corporation headquarters are located at:

1201 New York Ave. NW
Washington, DC 20525

Introduction

Name (First, Middle, Last)   Age   **AmeriCorps Referral Form**

Address

City/County   State   Zip

Telephone Day (   )   Evening (   )   Social Security Number

Send me:
❑ The listing of all
   AmeriCorps programs.
❑ Recruiting brochure and application for
   AmeriCorps *NCCC
❑ Recruiting brochure and application for
   AmeriCorps *VISTA

**I want to be in your database. Here's
some interesting information on me:
I am interested in serving in:**
❑ Full-time
   AmeriCorps programs
   (from 9 months to a year)
❑ Part-time
   AmeriCorps programs
**For More Information,
Call: 1-800-94-ACORPS
(1-800-942-2677)
TDD 1-800-833-3722**

Geographic Preference
❑ Programs in my area
❑ Anywhere in the U.S.A.
❑ Specific State *(specify)*

Specific Region
❑ Midwest
❑ Northeast
❑ Northwest
❑ Southeast
❑ Southwest

Specific Area Type
❑ Rural
❑ Urban
❑ No Preference

Earliest Date Available
____ September/Year ____
____ January/Year ____
____ June/Year ____
Other
Month __ Year __

Qualifications/Experience
Highest educational level attained
*(Check all that apply and list
major/field of study.)*
❑ Post Graduate Work *(specify)*
❑ MBA ❑ MD ❑ MSW
❑ JD   ❑ RN
❑ Other, *specify*

❑ Bachelor's Degree
❑ Some College
❑ Associate's Degree
❑ High School Diploma
❑ Some High School

Languages other than English
(specify)

Are you a U.S. Citizen or a Permanent
Resident Alien?
❑ Yes   ❑ No

Have you ever performed community service?

❑ Full-time   ❑ Part-time

Have you ever been in a National Service program?

❑ U.S. Armed Forces
   Currently in ___ *(Branch)*
   Honorably Discharged on
   _____ *(Date)*
❑ VISTA
❑ Peace Corps
❑ Other, *specify*

___

Skills *(check all that apply)*
❑ Computer
❑ Business/Managing/Accounting
❑ Public Speaking
❑ Mediation/Conflict Resolution
❑ Health
❑ Construction
❑ Community Outreach
❑ Landscaping/Gardening
❑ Child Development
❑ Teaching/Tutoring
❑ Counseling
❑ Writing
❑ Architecture/Design
❑ Victim Assistance
❑ Other, *specify*

___

Have you ever been employed?
❑ Full-time
❑ Part-time
❑ No

Do you have Experience (E) (paid or volunteer) and or specific Interest (I) in any of the following areas.

Place an E or I next to all that apply.
___ Early Childhood Development
___ Community Development
___ Education
___ Urban Environment
___ Literacy
___ Natural Resources
___ Health
___ Youth
___ Homelessness/Hunger
___ Crime Control/Prevention
Other, *specify*

___

Providing the following information is optional.
1. Describe your ethnic background
❑ African American
❑ Hispanic/Latino
❑ American Indian/Alaskan Native
❑ White non-Hispanic
❑ Asian American/Pacific Islander
❑ Other

___

2. Do you have any physical or mental disabilities that may require accommodation?
❑ Yes   ❑ No

3. Gender   ❑ M   ❑ F

4. Does your family receive public assistance (AFDC, Food Stamps)?
❑ Yes, *specify*   ❑ No

___

Total household income from all sources
$_____

How many people (parents, siblings, children) live with you?
_____

Profiles

Learning from the Dreamers
By Kevin Y. Riley, I Have a Dream Foundation

I am a full-time AmeriCorps volunteer with the *I Have a Dream Foundation* in my hometown of Chicago. As an Assistant Project Coordinator for the Goudy site, I work with a group of 35 eighth graders from low-income families in the Uptown neighborhood. Working out of a Boys and Girls Club, our project offers the "Dreamers" a daily array of activities which include tutoring, mentoring, recreation and leadership opportunities. The sponsor of our project, Leonard Herman, has promised each of these young men and women a college scholarship when they graduate from high school. This promise gives the kids a chance to have goals and aspirations that might otherwise not have seemed possible. Then the program helps each Dreamer develop the academic and social skills they will need to achieve those dreams.

Along with the part-time AmeriCorps volunteer, Christie Breen, I have been challenged with specific responsibilities during our year of service. First, we are in the process of expanding and further structuring the tutoring and mentoring program already in place. Before our kids can start planning for college, they have to graduate from high school. To that end, we have recruited over 30 new volunteers to help us out. These dedicated individuals include students from Northwestern and Loyola University, as well as young processionals from a variety of fields. Christie and I have also had to brush up on improper fractions and run-on sentences to full our role as live-in, de facto tutors.

The second major focus of our work this year is engaging the Dreamers in community service and service learning. Through informal surveys of fellow Dreamers and their parents, the group decided that we would like to develop initiatives to help out senior citizens in the community. The highlight of our fall program was the snowy Friday evening in December that we spent caroling at a local nursing home. Striding through the halls, bellowing offbeat notes and handing out candycanes to the residents, the Dreamers, parents, and volunteers were rewarded with appreciative smiles and generous applause. The following week we hosted a conference with another *IHAD* project where we discussed issues regarding the care of senior citizens in our communities and within our own families. This spring we have launched an Adopt-a-Grandparent program where our Dreamers are establishing friendships with senior citizens from nursing homes in the local community.

Kevin Riley (far left) with Project Coordinator Ruben Anguiano and two "dreamers" on top of an element of a team building course at Camp Rosenthal in Dowagiac, Michigan.

AmeriCorps has been a unique and life-altering experience for me. Upon graduation from the University of Richmond in 1993, I had a vague notion about engaging myself in some meaningful endeavor for a few years while I fleshed out career plans. I had hoped to expand my horizons and maybe help out the world a little in the meantime. Ever since a semester internship on the Hill, I was inflicted with Potomac fever and impressed with the "importance" of it all. I thought that a job on a Congressional staff would be the place to get "important" things done that "made a difference."

Before I could get there, however, I was sidetracked into a seven month journey through Latin America. After a four-month stay in a village in the Guatemalan rainforest, I was inspired by the beauty of the land and the richness of the souls whom I encountered. I came back to the United States with serious thoughts about returning to work with the conservation organization Pro-Peten. This group is among those fighting to save the Peten, Central America's largest rainforest. I was particularly attracted to the organization's focus on the concerns of the Peten's native population and how they would affect the future of the forest.

In the summer following my return, I rekindled the house painting business that I had run throughout college. I spent many long days up on the ladder contemplating my future. After living among the descendants of the ancient Maya and feeling the joy of direct service to a noble cause, the pinstripes and policy lunches of the beltway had lost much of their luster. At the same time, another unfocused jaunt in the jungle was not offering much in the way of job skills. It was then that I head about AmeriCorps and *I Have a Dream*.

My experience to date has proven both personally enriching and professionally clarifying. Everyday that I spend with the Dreamers, I learn as much from them about myself and the way I see the world as they learn from the program.

With my AmeriCorps stipend, I am looking to begin an M.S.W. program in the fall of '96. In the meantime, after my year of service is completed, I hope to work in a residential home for troubled adolescents. I have a different idea now about what it means to be "important."

AmeriCorps *Vermont Fire Technical Support Team*

By Sharon S. Quinlan, Education/Marketing Specialist

Here is what Vergennes Assistant Fire Chief, Ray Davidson, has to say about the *Vermont Fire Technical Support Team*: "It took twenty years of letter writing and talking with officials to get the help the fire service so desperately needed." The *VFTST* is the result of a joint AmeriCorps grant applied for by USDA Natural Resources Conservation Service, the George D. Aiken and Northern Vermont Resource Conservation and Development Council, and the Rural Fire Protection Task Force. The Task Force developed a Vermont initiative that supports volunteer fire departments in their quest to provide maximum level of security against fire loss.

Working with the Task Force and its mission is the AmeriCorps *Vermont Fire Technical Support Team.* The *VFTST* is available to help communities develop emergency water supply plans, evaluate and design water withdrawal systems —including dry hydrants, cisterns, drafting basins; and to provide construction inspection of installed improvements. In combination with the technical help they provide, the team also provides education and marketing expertise to communities.

Seventy-two towns requested the team's assistance. The team will provide twenty Fire Protection Water Supply Plans to communities. These plans contain technical data about each town; surveys of ponds, lakes, streams; and designs for dry hydrants, cisterns, and drafting basins. The team also provides marketing, recruiting, fund raising, and grants support.

Matthew Calcagni, Thomas Page, and Sharon Quinlan of the Vermont Fire Technical Support Team.

The three member *VFTST* is comprised of Matthew J. Calcagni, Thomas A. Page, and Sharon S. Quinlan. Matt, Engineering Technical specialist, is evaluating and designing water withdrawal facilities. He is assisting communities with adherence to engineering standards and specifications. Matt is also assisting them with the installation of dry hydrant systems and drafting basins. He is a native of Barre, and has recently obtained an Associates Degree in Civil Engineering from Vermont Technical College.

Thomas A. Page has a B.S. in Environmental Resource Management from the Pennsylvania State University. Tom is the Team Coordinator and the person responsible for coordination, scheduling, and plan development.

Sharon S. Quinlan is the Education/Marketing Specialist for the team. She has a B.A. from the University of Maryland and is currently attending Norwich University studying Environmental Psychology. Sharon has 25 years of experience in marketing and design, working with such agencies as the Vermont Lottery as well as national and international corporations.

Her environmental studies, expertise in the design and engineering of ponds, and years of volunteer work influenced her to join the *VFTST*. Sharon believes that volunteer fire fighters make up the pinnacle of volunteerism. "Fire fighters are the only group of volunteers who risk their lives each time they respond to a call for help." Of her role with the *VFTST* she says, "It's the best job in the world."

Building the *Bridge to Independence*
By Cynthia Holden-Elk, Independence Assistant

Here in Western Pennsylvania we call them "tent worms." I'm not really sure what they are; they eventually turn into some sort of moth, mate, lay eggs, and die. In the interim, they have the ability to completely strip a full grown tree of its foliage and will drop from the trees into your hair without warning. Their appearance can only be described as furry and gross, and should you happen to step on one, be prepared for the mustard-green "ooze" they produce that could make even the strongest of stomachs turn.

As my roommate and I shared our morning coffee, tent worms were all I could think about. They had infested the sprawling crabapple trees on Mrs. W's front lawn. Upon the discovery of these parasites, Mrs. W broke down in tears of frustration. She was already overworked and overwhelmed. Tent worms were absolutely the last thing she needed to think about. This morning, I couldn't seem to get them off my mind.

"Let's get it done. Let's go burn the tent worms from Mrs. W's tree this morning." I was thinking aloud again, and my roommate Denny was listening. I was worried about Mrs. W; she was not her usual "perky" self yesterday when I visited. She was both physically and emotionally exhausted. Those horrid tent worms were the straw that broke the camel's back.

Before I knew it, we were standing on Mrs. W's sidewalk, falming torch in hand. You see, this was the only known remedy for these things we call tent worms. Our extermination completed, we visited briefly with Mrs. W and her son, who suffers from multiple sclerosis. Denny had brought along a new computer game for her son, to help develop his manual dexterity. We all laughed and talked while the game was loading onto the hard drive of their home computer.

As Mrs. W walked us to the door, she whispered to Denny, "Cynthia has been so good for my son." I pretended not hear their private exchange, but I'm sure I could not conceal how proud I was at that moment of my AmeriCorps service. She hugged us both and once again began to cry.

I saw the same look of personal pride and satisfaction mirrored back in my roommate's smile. This time he was thinking aloud, "When she started to cry, I thought something was wrong. Then I realized that she was just happy."

On the way home, I offered this explanation for my AmeriCorps service:

> *I visit Mrs. W and her son as an AmeriCorps member. I joined the Corps through the National Multiple Sclerosis Society. The program that NMSS has developed to utilize Corps members is the "Bridge to Independence." I serve as an Independence Assistant, offering a Home Companion/Chore Service designed to improve the quality of life for people who have multiple sclerosis and their families.*

Of course we accomplished more than just a chore that needed to be done this morning. Yesterday Mrs. W felt helpless and hopeless. Today she may still feel discouraged and faltering, but she realized that both help and hope exist.

The Todd Hamer Story: An All AmeriCorps Hero

California Commission on Improving Life through Service

Todd Hamer grew up in Los Milinos, California, a farming community in northern California. As a past student body president, an honors graduate and a full track scholarship to the University of Mines in Colorado, Todd was a young man with a future. With a little hard work, he was close to finishing his first year of college with a B average and three first place ribbons in track.

The same year, with the Mill Creek Park Mother's Day Picnic well underway, he and two buddies took off for a quick dip in the Sacramento River. Running and diving in head first the other young men cam up laughing—but not Todd. He was slumped over, bleeding and unconscious. Todd had broken his neck. The third and fourth vertebrae in his spine had been severed. After three week of hospitalization and six months of rehabilitation Todd was destined to be confined to a wheelchair for the rest of his life.

Wheelchair or not, Todd graduated from college with honors in 1992 with a degree in Geological Engineering. Just as he was about to begin his career the Watershed Project began to put together an AmeriCorps team to help implement a watershed education project in Tehama County. With his advanced knowledge of science and technology, he was sought after by the project director, who asked him to apply for a position as a site-based coordinator.

While Todd was reluctant to commit due to his disability,

he decided nevertheless to put his professional career on hold. He applied to the Watershed Project and was accepted. Today Todd continues to make a difference in Los Molinos High School where he works directly with teachers and students building watershed units in physics, natural resources, biology, and advanced math. He is an inspiration to students everyday as he demonstrates that physical challenges don't have to stand in the way of making a commitment to service.

Todd's wheelchair has not kept him from any field trips. Students enthusiastically "blaze" the trails for him, clearing brush so that he can maneuver his wheelchair through the wilderness. Tehama County is fortunate to have Todd and other AmeriCorps team members working on the Watershed project. National Service has provided a unique opportunity for people like Todd to not only share their knowledge but to serve as mentors and role models to youth across the nation. And finally, National Service is proving to be an able partner to public parks in their efforts to comply with the Americans with Disabilities Act (ADA).

PROGRAM SNAPSHOTS

Training to Reduce Violence Offered by *CAN*
By Lorrie B. Bentson, Executive Director

Preventing and reducing violence among youth, especially ages 10-15, is the focus of the AmeriCorps USA program developed by *Community Action of Nebraska, Inc. (CAN)*. CAN has placed its 23 AmeriCorps members in eight community action agencies around Nebraska. The AmeriCorps members are working directly with youth to prevent and reduce violence through peer mediation, conflict resolution training, and other programs targeted at youth. Many of the programs are operated in schools, and others are in settings such as after school programs, camps, youth shelters, and youth organizations. The program is touching the lives of literally thousands of youth through workshops on how to help each other resolve conflicts, and though a variety of specially tailored programs, such as one that has designed new playground rules and games to reduce fights on an elementary playground.

The AmeriCorps members received 46 hours of training in basic mediation and school mediation to prepare them for their assignments. Training was provided by the Nebraska Office of Dispute Resolution and the six regional mediation centers in the state. Additional training in public speaking, first aide, CPR, victim-offender mediation and job search skills is being offered. This level of training will be offered to the second year's class as well.

How It Works in Kansas City
By Ann Elizabeth Jurcyk, Program Director, United Way AmeriCorps

The *United Way Neighborhood Corps of Kansas City, Kansas* operates on an annual cycle of January through December. There are twenty-one full-time positions available. The Corps is divided into three teams that work in three inner city neighborhoods in Kansas City. The approach of our neighborhood revitalization efforts is based on a "capacity building model"—that of building on the existing strengths in the community to rebuild neighborhoods from the inside out. Working in conjunction with trusted neighborhood agencies called advisory boards, corpsmembers begin by surveying residents to learn what skills and attributes are present in the neighborhood. The results are presented in a townhall meeting. The corpsmembers then work to help residents design and implement projects and programs that build on these strengths and address the local concerns.

This program is ideal for anyone who exhibits responsibility and vision; candidates need to possess a willingness to take initiative, be able to work with a team, responsibly organize and lead others. Current corpsmembers enjoy many benefits: working under an established lead agency (United Way), the camaraderie of a cohesive crew, excellent training opportunities, as well as the latitude they are afforded to build on their own interests and strengths. Of course, there is also the satisfaction of seeing results such as immunization drives, beautification efforts, park revitalization, sports tournaments, community gardens, traffic signs put in, neighborhood watch groups, and others.

Business and Environmental Development
Southwest Oregon Resource Conservation & Development AmeriCorps Rural Development Program

The *Southwest Oregon Resource Conservation & Development/AmeriCorps Rural Development Program* consists of five members. Working with watershed groups in the Rogue Basin, Curry County, and Coquille watershed, three members have lent a hand with watershed assessments, project development, grant writing, education and landowner involvement. In Douglas County, two AmeriCorps members work with local economic development groups to develop and implement strategic plans, support local businesses, and improve community livability.

As an example of local economic development, Pat McVean is working in the North County Economic Development (NCED). She has B.A. in Recreation Leisure Services, with an emphasis in management of municipal facilities and therapeutic recreation. She is working as coordinator of NCED, a grassroots organization whose goal is to enhance the quality of life in the area through capacity building and planned economic growth and diversification. NCED projects include a multi-purpose community center, city restrooms, topographic survey, sewer district formation and highway planning.

Education on Battle Mountain

Battle Mountain Band AmeriCorps Educational Program; Battle Mountain Indian Colony, Nevada

The mission of this program is to improve the level of educational achievement of the Battle Mountain Band's members through an extensive tutoring, enrichment, and outreach program. Even though this concept has been introduced elsewhere, it is an entirely new and innovative concept for this community. This year-long project is a pilot program

The Battle Mountain Band is one of four bands of the Te-Moak Tribe of Western Shoshone, a federally recognized Indian Tribe. The Battle Mountain Band colonies are located in rural Northern Nevada. Due to the small size of the community, one fulltime (Head Tutor) and two part-time AmeriCorps members are employed. The Head Tutor develops learning programs, working directly with children and administering the program. For the AmeriCorps member, this provides career experience in education and counseling. The Corpsmember is encouraged to take courses relating to child development.

Combating Poverty in Rural Arkansas
USDA Rural Economic and Community Development Service

USDA Rural Economic and Community Development Service in Arkansas has six AmeriCorps participants. They are providing assistance to the applicants of the Empowerment Zone/Enterprise Community Initiative in Eastern Arkansas. The strategic plans for this program was developed following town hall meetings held last year to express the concerns of the community as a whole and share a vision for the future. Needs range from the creation of literacy programs, shelters, mentoring programs, promoting construction and rehabilitation of street and drainage systems, water and sewer systems, counseling programs, health care reform, job creation, and housing needs.

So far the participants have studied grant writing and have assisted communities in filing applications to the state and federal government for programs. Housing needs have been identified, drug awareness and teen pregnancy programs have been provided to schools. The participants have gained knowledge of their communities and become aware of many programs and resources that can benefit their communities for many years to come. Most of all these participants have learned the personal benefit that can be gained from giving of themselves.

An AmeriCorps member with the Watershed Project AmeriCorps program in Northern California with students from the Los Molinos Unified School District. Kindergarten children were planting willow sticks to aid in erosion control in Dye Creek, at the Gray Davis Nature Conservancy.

Participants and team members of the Children of the Future Program, *adminis- tered by the Greater Columbus Arts Coun- cil in cooperation with the City of Columbus Recreation and Parks Department, the City of Columbus Depart- ment of Safety, and the Columbus Metro- politan Housing Authority. Photo- graph by Chas Krider.*

Volunteer Anne-Edington Jenkins at a Head Start Program operated by the opportunity corporation of Madison & Buncombe Counties, Asheville, NC.

AmeriCorps members in Cleveland, Ohio, being sworn in by President Clinton via satellite.

AmeriCorps volunteers in the Class-MATES (Mentors and Tutors Enhancing Schools) AmeriCorps Project in Cleveland, Ohio.

Directory of State Contacts and Programs

The Corporation for National Service
General Information: 202/606-5000

This directory was compiled from information provided by the Corporation for National Service and the state commissions. If contact names and phone or fax numbers have changed, contact the state commission or the Corporation. Application procedures may be found on page x of the Introduction.

ALABAMA

State Lead Contact:

Ms. E. Elaine Wiggins
Governor's Office on National and
Community Service
224 The Alabama Statehouse
11 S. Union Street
Montgomery, AL 36130
Phone: 205/242-7174
Fax: 205/242-2885

Co-Director:

Mr. Jack Timmons
State Program Director
The Corporation for National Service
600 Beacon Parkway West
Birmingham, AL 35209-3120
Phone: 205/290-7184
Fax: 205/290-7186

1995-96 Programs

National Service Network

AL-1

Statewide:
Program: HHS—Administration on Developmental Disabilities
AmeriCorps Members: 70 (Nationally)
Description: AmeriCorps Members will provide personal assistance services to increase the social and economic independence of individuals with developmental disabilities.
Contact: Ellen Dossett; 205/934-2965

AL-2

Birmingham:
Program: University of Alabama at Birmingham School of Public Health/AmeriCorps Health and Housing Program Fellows
AmeriCorps Members: 4 (31 Nationally)
Description: Four public health colleges (University of Alabama at Birmingham, Johns Hopkins, Boston University, University of El Paso) joined to create the Health and Housing Fellows program. Taking an innovative approach to community-based public health, the program enrolls Returned Peace Corps Volunteers (RPVC's) as AmeriCorps members who will serve for two years while studying for a master's degree in public health or nursing at the University of Alabama. With the guidance of faculty mentors, members will perform a community health needs assessment from which they will design, implement, and evaluate public health projects in the areas of AIDS and infectious disease, teen pregnancy, violence, and substance abuse.
Contact: David Coombs; 205/934-6020; 205/934-9325 (fax)

AL-3

Birmingham:
Program: National Community AIDS Partnership (NCAP)/"Youth & HIV/AIDS Services Partnership"
AmeriCorps Members: 8 (40 Nationally)
Description: NCAP is dedicated to supporting high-quality education and service initiatives to fight the HIV/AIDS epidemic in the United States. AmeriCorps Members will provide direct care and assistance to HIV victims and offer education for high-risk communities.
Contact: Harry L. Brown; 205/251-5131; 205/323-8730

AL-4

Birmingham:
Program: Youth Volunteer Corps of America/YVCA Leadership Corps
AmeriCorps Members: 8 (107 Nationally)
Description: AmeriCorps Members will develop, run, and enroll volunteers in service projects including: summer camps, academic enrichment programs, service-learning curricula, conflict resolution training, gang alternative programs, and identification of high crime areas.
Contact: Kenneth Cunningham; 205/970-0251; 205/970-0349 (fax)

State and Local

AL-5

Birmingham:
Program: Birmingham AIDS Outreach/BAO AmeriCorps
AmeriCorps Members:
Description: During their full year of service, AmeriCorps members will provide home health care and assistance to people living with AIDS to reduce the exorbitant costs of hospitals and health care that overwhelm AIDS patients and their families and to help AIDS patients maintain their independence. Following a year of service, members will return to their college campuses to share their experiences and provide peer education on AIDS prevention.
Contact: Mr. Terry Gunnell; 205/322-4197 025/320-1279

AL-6

Montgomery:
Program: YMCA/Changing Lives AmeriCorps
AmeriCorps Members:
Description: Taking a comprehensive approach to poverty in Southeast Alabama, AmeriCorps members will tutor low-income parents to become children's first teachers, will tutor juvenile court referrals to help them stay in school, will lead juvenile court referrals and other interested youth in community service projects, will provide elementary and high-risk youth with outdoor leadership training, will provide health education and government education to rural youth, and will help teen mothers gain access to health care.
Contact: Patrick Enfinger; 334/269-4362; 334/269-4836 (fax)

AL-7

Auburn:
Program: Alabama Council on Human Relations (ACHR)/Communities in Action
AmeriCorps Members:
Description: To break the cycle of intergenerational poverty and dependency on federal assistance, AmeriCorps members will provide the following services to single parents with children in Head Start or daycare: enroll parents in G.E.D. classes, tutor parents, assist parents in securing jobs and adequate housing, teach parents about financial management, advocate for parents' needs in community, encourage and coordinate parent coalitions and support groups for low income families.
Contact: Roberta Jackel; 205/821-8336; 205/826-6397

AL-8

Dothan:
Program: Troy State University at Dothan/One Problem at a Time (OPT)
AmeriCorps Members:
Description: To reduce the problem of violence and crime (particularly youth-oriented), AmeriCorps members will lead youth corps of children and teens to: 1) identify public safety problems in their community, 2) develop projects to address those problems, and 3) implement the projects that the young people initiated and planned.
Contact: Dr. Francina Williams; 205/712-0010; 205/983-6322 (fax)

AL-9

Tuscaloosa:
Program: University of Alabama/Students for Alabama Independent Living (SAIL)
Description: AmeriCorps members will assist disabled individuals to improve their self-sufficiency, productivity, and independence by providing the following: limited physical therapy, home facilities upgrading for handicapped accessibility,

assistance in school enrollment and securing employment, tutoring, and general advocacy. *Contact:* Valerie Phillips or Nikki Craft; 205/348-6114; 205/348-7610 (fax)

ALASKA

State Lead Contact:

Edgar Blatchford
Commissioner
Department of Regional and Community Affairs
P.O. 112100
Juneau, AK 99801
Phone: 907/465-4700
Fax: 907/465-2948

State Commission:

Alaska National Community Service Commission

1995-96 Programs

National Service Network

AK-1

Anchorage:
Program: Environmental Protection Agency/Improving Disadvantaged Neighborhoods
AmeriCorps Members: 15
Description: Responding to a solid waste and sanitation crisis in Native American villages, AmeriCorps Members will work with local planners and community-based organizations to develop and implement waste management strategies and to conduct a solid waste education program.
Contact: Helga Butler; 202/260-4179

AK-2

Anchorage:
Program: Nine Star Enterprises, Inc.
AmeriCorps Members:
Description: Nine Star programs support and instruct adult literacy and basic education for students, tutors, instructors, and administrators. Americorps Members serve families through family literacy instruction and senior citizens through tutoring provided to older Alaskans. Members both tutor new adult red-

ers and recruit new volunteers to expand existing literacy work in Alaskan communities.
Contact: Mr. David Alexander; 907/563-3174

AK-3

Anchorage:
Program: RurAL Cap
AmeriCorps Members:
Description: AmeriCorps members will address early childhood development, mental illness and homelessness, and substance abuse needs of Native Alaskans. Members will work as teachers' aides in Head Start programs, mental health counselors, and facilitators for a homelessness prevention initiative.
Contact: Ms. Jeanine Kennedy; 907/279-2511; 907/278-2309 (fax)

AK-4

Juneau:
Program: Southeast Alaska Guidance Association (SAGA)
AmeriCorps Members:
Description: AmeriCorps Members from diverse Alaskan communities will conserve the environment, rehabilitate affordable housing, lead over 200 K-12 students in direct service projects, and deliver substance abuse, teen pregnancy, and teen suicide workshops to K-12 students.
Contact: Ms. Donna DeBoer -Williams; 907/789-6172; 907/789-3118 (fax)

ARIZONA

State Lead Contact:

Jaime Molera
AZ National and Community Service Commission
1700 W. Washington St., 3d Floor
Phoenix, AZ 85007
Phone: 602/542-3461
Fax: 602/542-3520

1995-96 Programs

National Service Network

AZ-1

Statewide:
(Rural areas)
Program: USDA Rural Development Team
AmeriCorps Members: 50 (Four Corners)
Description: AmeriCorps Members will help communities protect watersheds, improve housing, promote economic development, boost sustainable agriculture and respond to disasters.
Contact: Bonnie Fricks; 520/281-1068

AZ-2

Program: USDA Public Lands and Environment Team
AmeriCorps Members: 45 (564 Nationally)
Description: As part of an effort to restore public lands and reduce community environmental hazards, AmeriCorps Members will improve, build, and staff camping and recreational facilities.
Contact: Joel Berg; 202/720-6350

AZ-3

Phoenix:
Program: Acorn Housing Corporation/A Home for All
Description: AmeriCorps Members increase home ownership opportunities through their work as intake and loan counselors. They also conduct community workshops and provide pre-purchase counseling to individual clients.
Contact: Sabrina Garcia; 602/253-1111; 602/258-7143 (fax)

AZ-4

Phoenix:
Program: Teach for America/The Next Stage
AmeriCorps Members: 20 (1000 Nationally)
Description: AmeriCorps Members will respond to an acute need for educators and role models in under-served urban and rural areas by introducing innovative teaching methods to the classroom.
Contact: Lisa Morehouse; 602/954-9777; 602/954-9917

AZ-5

Tucson:
Program: Arizona Mexico Commission/Border Volunteer Corps
Description: AmeriCorps Members provide service activities including transporting mothers and children to immunization clinics, training farm workers in pesticide safety, and teaching family literacy and English as a second language.
Contact: Issa Carrazco; 602/326-1774; 800/320-1774; 602/326-1759

AZ-6

Tucson:
Program: National Center for Family Literacy—The Family Literacy Corps
Description: AmeriCorps Members work with undereducated parents and pre-school children, serving as early childhood, adult education, and/or social service assistants. Members help with home visits, recruitment, tutoring of school-age children, and summer enrichment activities.
Contact: Jessica Dilworth; 602/889-9962

AZ-7

Tucson:
Program: Youth Volunteer Corps of America/YVCA Leadership Corps
AmeriCorps Members: 15 (107 Nationally)
Description: AmeriCorps Members will develop, run, and enroll volunteers in service projects including: summer camps, academic enrichment programs, service-learning curricula, conflict resolution training, gang alternative programs, and identification of high crime areas.
Contact: Jennifer Gilmore; 520/886-6500; 520/722-6066

AZ-8

Window Rock:
Program: Navajo Nation Youth Conservation Corps
AmeriCorps Members: 40 (120 Nationally)
Description: Building self-esteem in "at-risk" youth takes a decidedly environmental slant with community revitalization projects focused on watershed and soil conservation using both western and traditional Navajo

technologies.

Contact: Elizabeth Washburne; 602/871-6605; 602/871-5493

· *State and Local*

AZ-9

Flagstaff:

Program: Youth In Action/Northern Arizona University

AmeriCorps Members: 40

Description: AmeriCorps Members will be placed in elementary schools and high schools to tutor and mentor at-risk students, teach computer skills and arts and crafts, organize recreational activities, and train volunteers to provide after-school substance abuse prevention training for at-risk elementary school students.

Contact: Ms. Kathy Dunn Turner; 520/523-2199; 520/523-6395 (fax)

AZ-10

Mesa:

Program: City of Mesa

AmeriCorps Members: 20

Description: AmeriCorps Members will reduce gang activity by working with police to provide gang resistance presentations to the community, tutoring at-risk youth and first offenders, disseminating public safety-related information, and assisting welfare recipients to become self-sufficient.

Contact: Ms. Mary Hutchinson; 602/252-9363; 602/252-8664 (fax)

AZ-11

Phoenix:

Program: Arizona Council of Centers for Children & Adults—ACCCA

AmeriCorps Members: 21

Description: AmeriCorps Members will be placed in education and health services organizations to mentor at-risk youth and adults, assistant teach in a Head Start program, and function as assistant social workers in an early intervention/family support services program.

Contact: Stacey Gubser; 602/252-9363; 800/506-1444; 602/252-8664 (fax)

AZ-12

Phoenix:

Program: Arizona Conservation Corps/Arizona Conservation Corps Leadership Corps Proposal

AmeriCorps Members: 52

Description: AmeriCorps Members will protect the environment and improve low-income housing by preserving land, water, flora, and wildlife, and by weatherizing and rehabilitating homes for low-income and former homeless people.

Contact: Mr. Larry Hand; 602/254-1810; 602/258-0504 (fax)

AZ-13

Tucson:

Program: Arizona AHEC Rural AmeriCorps Program

AmeriCorps Members: 20

Description: AmeriCorps Members will improve primary health care for low-income mothers and their families by providing health education, ensuring health screening and follow-up care, and assisting local schools in establishing health career and mentorship programs.

Contact: Mr. Donald Proulx; Ms. Nancy Collyer; 520/626-7946; 520/326-6429 (fax)

ARKANSAS

State Lead Contact:

Betty Hicks
Arkansas Division of Volunteerism
P.O. Box 1437
Slot 1300
Little Rock, AR 72203
Phone: 501/682-7540
Fax: 501/682-6752

1995-96 Programs

National Service Network

AR-1

Statewide:
(Rural areas)

Program: Association of Farmworkers Opportunity Program

AmeriCorps Members: 5 (61 Nationally)
Description: AmeriCorps Members will train migrant and seasonal farmworkers on how to reduce exposure to pesticides and improve farmworkers' access to other health, education and support services.
Contact: Clevon Young; 501/374-1103

AR-2

Program: Delta Service Corps
AmeriCorps Members: 145 (435 Nationally)
Description: Through a partnership with local community agencies, AmeriCorps Members will assist low-income residents in finding affordable housing, tutor children to enhance their literacy skills and work with state parks to conserve and restore the environment.
Contact: Jeff Crawford; 501/897-5566

AR-3

Program: USDA Rural Development Team
AmeriCorps Members: 67 (Mississippi Delta)
Description: AmeriCorps Members will help communities protect watersheds, improve housing, promote economic development, boost sustainable agriculture and respond to disasters.
Contact: Shirley Tucker; 501/324-6284

AR-4

Program: USDA/Forestry Service/Soil Conservation Service
AmeriCorps Members: 14
Description: Contact the Arkansas Commission on National and Community Service for further information: 501/682-6724.
Contact: Tomas Dominguez; 501/324-5444

State and Local

AR-5

Texarkana:
Program: School-Based Truancy Project/ Arkansas Family Network
AmeriCorps Members: 12
Description: Members increase educational achievements if students and improve relationships with students, parents, faculty, etc.
Contact: Joe Owens; 501/774-3161

AR-6

Conway and Perry Counties:
Program: Community Alliance for a Safe Tomorrow (CAST Out the Violence)
AmeriCorps Members: 21 full-time; 11 part-time
Description: Members help reduce youth crime and violence.
Contact: Robin Hayes; 501/450-3194

AR-7

Warren:
Program: POP'S Latchkey Program
AmeriCorps Members: 10
Description: Addresses issues of family management and academic failure in early childhood. AmeriCorps members interact with children preparing and participating in age-appropriate activities with them while teaching and modeling proper behavior.
Contact: Mrs. Audrey Raines; 501/226-6920

CALIFORNIA

State Lead Contact:

Dr. Linda Forsyth
California Commission on Improving Life Through Service
1121 L St., Suite 600
Sacramento, CA 95814
Phone: 916/327-4836
Fax: 916/323-3227

1995-96 Programs

National Service Network

CA-1

Statewide:
(Rural areas)
Program: Association of Farmworkers Opportunity Program
AmeriCorps Members: 28 (61 Nationally)
Description: AmeriCorps Members will train migrant and seasonal farmworkers on how to reduce exposure to pesticides and improve farmworkers' access to other health, education and support services.
Contact: Paul Castro; 209/466-3053; 209/ 466-5546 (fax)

CA-2

Statewide:
Program: USDA Rural Development Team
AmeriCorps Members: 30 AmeriCorps
Members
Description: AmeriCorps Members will
repair and protect burned watersheds, protect
critical individual species, supervise tree
planting and erosion control.
Contact: Tim Cattron; 916/757-8300

CA-3

Northern Areas:
Program: USDA Public Lands and Environment Team
AmeriCorps Members: 20 (564 Nationally)
Description: As part of an effort to reduce
public lands and reduce community environmental hazards, AmeriCorps Members will
improve, build, and staff camping and recreational facilities.
Contact: Tony Montana; 707/441-3555; 707/
442-9242 (fax)

CA-4

Southern Areas:
Program: USDA Public Lands and Environment Team
AmeriCorps Members: 77 (564 Nationally)
Description: As part of an effort to reduce
public lands and reduce community environmental hazards, AmeriCorps Members will
improve, build, and staff camping and recreational facilities.
Contact: Terry Murphy; 909/794-6198; 909/
794-1125 (fax)

CA-5

Southern Areas:
Program: Department of the Interior/South-
ern California Urban Water Conservation
program
AmeriCorps Members: 15 (505 Nationally)
Description: Working with the Bureau of
Reclamation and the Metropolitan Water
District, AmeriCorps Members will educate
communities about water conservation and
act on their suggestions by implementing
household projects. The goal is to reduce residential water consumption by 150 million
gallons annually.

Contact: Kourt D. Williams; 310/660-0280;
310/660-0282 (fax)

CA-6

Statewide:
Program: National Association of Child
Care Resource and Referral Agencies/Action
for Children Today! (ACT)
AmeriCorps Members: 15 (45 Nationally)
Description: AmeriCorps Members will educate the community about child care needs
and increase child care availability by training staff and opening centers.
Contact: Jan Brown; 213/427-2755; 213/
427-2756 (fax)

CA-7

Santa Cruz:
Program: Department of the Interior/Ft. Ord
Habitat Restoration
AmeriCorps Members: 20 (505 Nationally)
Description: AmeriCorps Members will
work on this military-based conversion
project restoring wildlife habitat, construct-
ing erosion controls and rehabilitating trails.
Contact: Brenda Herrmann; 408/475-1131;
408/475-8350 (fax)

CA-8

Inglewood:
Program: Children's Health Fund/Ameri-
Corps Community Outreach
AmeriCorps Members: 3 (15 Nationally)
Description: The Children's Health Fund
was designed to meet the complex health
care needs of medically under-served, homeless, and impoverished children. AmeriCorps
Members will encourage families to take
advantage of available primary health care
resources.
Contact: Chynethia Leak; 310/412-3737;
310/674-1578 (fax)

CA-9

Los Angeles:
Program: US Department of Justice/Opera-
tion Weed & Seed "Just Serve"
AmeriCorps Members: 30
Description: AmeriCorps Members will
teach crime prevention to children through
conflict resolution techniques. The program
will enhance neighborhood environments

through empowerment strategies such as linking police and neighborhood residents through law enforcement, community policing, prevention, intervention, treatment and economic revitalization.
Contact: Amy Miller; 213/753-4551; 213/751-2801 (fax)

CA-10

Los Angeles:
Program: Green Corps' Neighborhood Green Corps Program
AmeriCorps Members: 20
Description: Splitting their time between projects involving the home environment and the community environment, Ameri-Corps Members will educate and then activate their communities through three projects: low income home weatherization, lead paint abatement, and urban gardening.
Contact: Susan Comfort; 415/441-7823; 415/441-7826 (fax)

CA-11

Statewide:
Program: Teach for America—The Next Stage
AmeriCorps Members: 258
Description: AmeriCorps Members will respond to an acute need for educators and role models in under-served urban and rural areas by lending their diverse perspectives on education while introducing innovative teaching methods to the classroom.
Contact: Southern: Gregory Good; 310/648-0077; 310/648-0140 (fax); Northern: Anna Johnson; 510/444-2377; 510/444-2303 (fax)

CA-12

Los Angeles:
Program: USDA Anti-Hunger Team
AmeriCorps Members: 40 (150 Nationally)
Description: Several local service agencies will join AmeriCorps Members in performing outreach for food assistance programs. Efforts will focus on increasing use of the Summer Food Service in Los Angeles public schools and on establishing farmers' markets for low-income residents.
Contact: Liz Riley; 213/913-7333 ext 14; 213/664-1725 (fax)

CA-13

Los Angeles:
Program: Department of Veterans Affairs/Homeless Vets
AmeriCorps Members: 14
Description: AmeriCorps Members will help homeless veterans obtain needed medical care, drug abuse prevention and treatment, as well as vocational training.
Contact: Stephanie Hardy; 310/348-7600; 310/641-2661 (fax)

CA-14

Sacramento:
Program: Summerbridge AmeriCorps Teaching Program
AmeriCorps Members: 68 Nationally
Description: AmeriCorps Members will recruit high school and college students to teach disadvantaged middle school students. The objectives are to improve students' academic and leadership performance and to build the members' commitment to a career in teaching.
Contact: Heather Hughes, Gina Duran; 916/481-8811

CA-15

Sacramento:
Program: AIDS Partnership (NCAP)/ "Youth & HIV/AIDS Services Partnership"
AmeriCorps Members: 8 (40 Nationally)
Description: NCAP is dedicated to supporting high-quality education and service initiatives to fight the HIV/AIDS epidemic in the United States. AmeriCorps Members will provide direct care and assistance to HIV victims and offer education for high-risk communities.
Contact: Peter Simpson; 916/368-3188; 916/368-3060 (fax)

CA-16

Santa Clara:
Program: National Multiple Sclerosis Society/"Bridge to Independence"
AmeriCorps Members: 8 (144 Nationally)
Description: AmeriCorps Members, many of who have Multiple Sclerosis, will work to build awareness about Multiple Sclerosis while coordinating volunteers in extensive

living assistance programs—helping disadvantaged people to make it on their own.
Contact: Denise Casey; 408/988-7557; 408/988-1816 (fax)

CA-17

San Rafael:
Program: Summerbridge AmeriCorps Teaching Program
AmeriCorps Members: 68 Nationally
Description: AmeriCorps Members will recruit high school and college students to teach disadvantaged middle school students. The objective will be to improve their academic and leadership performance.
Contact: Katie Graham; 415/456-4833

CA-18

Oakland, Richmond, San Pablo:
Program: Environmental Protection Agency—Neighborhood Improvement Project
AmeriCorps Members: 40
Description: AmeriCorps members will restore the national environment of urban waterways, perform radon testing, and provide training on techniques to prevent lead poisoning.
Contact: Joanna Lennon; 510/891-3900; 510/272-9001 (fax)

CA-19

San Francisco-San Jose:
Program: Environmental Careers Organization, Inc.—Technical Advisor Program for Toxics Use Reduction
AmeriCorps Members: 2
Description: AmeriCorps Members will serve communities by researching toxic chemical substitute; interpreting technical documents and data; performing non-regulatory facility evaluations to identify reduction opportunities; and assisting citizen groups in developing "Good Neighbor Agreements" with local manufacturing facilities. Members will receive ongoing training on current toxics use reduction methods and technologies.
Contact: Diane Mailey; 617/426-4375; 617/423-0998 (fax)

CA-20

San Francisco:
Program: National Endowment for the Arts/The Writers Corps
AmeriCorps Members: 20 (25 Nationally)
Description: AmeriCorps Members will work with homeless and runaway youth in creative writing and poetry workshops in order to improve writing and verbal skills, while boosting self-worth.
Contact: Janet Heller; 415/252-2546; 415/252-2595 (fax)

CA-21

San Francisco:
Program: Summerbridge AmeriCorps Teaching Program
AmeriCorps Members: 68 Nationally
Description: AmeriCorps Members will recruit high school and college students to teach disadvantaged middle school students. The objective will be to improve their academic and leadership performance.
Contact: San Francisco Day School: Al Gonzales, Anthony Thomas; 415/931-2422; San Francisco University High School: Tara Phillips; 415/749-2036

CA-22

San Francisco:
Program: YMCA Earth Service Corps Fellowship
AmeriCorps Members: 40 Nationally
Description: AmeriCorps Members will address local environmental concerns, coordinating park cleanups, urban gardening projects, and environmental symposia.
Contact: Northern: Chip Rich, Bob Tench; 415/286-9622; 415/286-0128 (fax); Southern: Dan Powell; 805/687-7727; 805/687-7568

CA-23

San Jose:
Program: City Year, Inc.
AmeriCorps Members: 55 (220 Nationally)
Description: Teams of AmeriCorps Members will take a holistic approach toward addressing seemingly unrelated community needs including: violence prevention, neighborhood environment, school success and

community revitalization.
Contact: Sabrina Gee; 408/294-3041; 408/
294-0615 (fax)

CA-24

San Joaquin County:
Program: Magic Me America
AmeriCorps Members: 11
Description: AmeriCorps Members will
orchestrate self-esteem building and academically motivating service-learning projects
directed at adolescents while serving isolated
elderly people.
Contact: Diana Fazzio; 209/468-4000; 209/
468-4040 (fax)

CA-25

Los Angeles:
Program: Legal Service Corporation/
National Service Legal Corps
AmeriCorps Members: 5
Description: AmeriCorps Members will
focus on community economic development
efforts which benefit at-risk youth and young
adults through job-training, gang intervention, literacy projects, and other programs.
Contact: Mary Ochs; 213/971-4102 ext. 423;
213/971-0314 (fax)

CA-26

Los Angeles:
Program: Family Literacy Corps
Description: AmeriCorps Members will
teach adults and children how to read.
Contact: Leandra Woods, Dolores Carrey;
213/264-4057; 213/264-1937 (fax)

CA-27

Los Angeles, Pasadena, Vallejo:
Program: The Neighborhood Reinvestment
Corporation/NeighborWorks Community
Corps
AmeriCorps Members: 12
Description: The NeighborWorks Community Corps, with which AmeriCorps Members will work, promotes neighborhood
stabilization through home ownership and
crime prevention. AmeriCorps Members will
assist with mortgage financing, work to
establish Neighborhood Watch groups, and
organize community rehabilitation in needy
cities throughout the country.

Contact: Donna Wright; 213/252-7658; 213/
252-7709 (fax)

CA-28

Program: Local Initiatives Support Corpora-
tion/LISC AmeriCorps
AmeriCorps Members: 34
Description: AmeriCorps Members will
work in community development corporations and engage in community revitalization
activities including housing, outreach, and
education, job training, community policing,
youth education, and other human services.
Contact: John Peroni, Andrea Phillips; 212/
455-9308; 212/682-5929 (fax)

CA-29

Statewide:
Program: Department of Interior/Earth Science Field Corps
AmeriCorps Members: 75
Description: AmeriCorps Members will
assist the U.S. Geological Survey in updating
geologic, geographic, and hydrologic information.
Contact: Susan Murphy; 415/329-4110; 415/
329-5497 (fax)

State and Local

CA-30

San Luis Obispo:
Program: RSVP AmeriCorps
AmeriCorps Members:
Description: AmeriCorps Members will
transform a Retired Senior Volunteer Pro-
gram into a center to develop and monitor
community service projects for AmeriCorps
Members.
Contact: Ms. Dale Magee; 805/549-7890;
805/549-7899 (fax)

CA-31

El Centro:
Program: Imperial County Office of Educa-
tion/Project AEGIS (Against Crime: Education Group for an Intervention System)
AmeriCorps Members:
Description: Planning grant to develop a
program in which AmeriCorps Members will
reduce community crime and school violence and improve health conditions of chil-

dren and families in two remote, economically disadvantaged areas of the county.
Contact: Ms. Rita Brogan; 619/339-6498; 619/353-3865 (fax)

CA-32

Escondido:
Program: Escondido Empowerment Corps
AmeriCorps Members: 30
Description: AmeriCorps Members will implement a public safety plan developed by a community partnership in the City of Escondido. Members will mentor youth, develop mediation programs, and organize neighborhood watch groups.
Contact: Ms. Kitty Burbridge; 619/747-6281; 619/747-1635 (fax)

CA-33

Eureka:
Program: Redwood Community Action Agency/Youth Reaching Youth
AmeriCorps Members:
Description: Planning grant will build partnerships to address the needs of educating youth and ensuring public safety in Humboldt County. AmeriCorps Members will develop and provide youth-oriented activities within ethnic and other community neighborhoods (schools, malls, neighborhood centers),
Contact: Ms. Susanne Hendry; 707/445-0881; 707/445-0884 (fax)

CA-34

Fortuna:
Program: California Conservation Corps/ The Watershed Stewards Project
AmeriCorps Members: 43
Description: AmeriCorps Members will use state-of-the-art monitoring techniques to analyze the health of watersheds and streams. Members will also organize watershed restoration efforts which will involve schools and community in tree planting; barrier modification; and gathering stream flow, rainfall, and temperature data.
Contact: Mr. Melvin Kreb; 707/725-8601; 707/725-8602 (fax)

CA-35

Hayfork:
Program: California Conservation Corps/ W.A.T.E.R Shed Project
AmeriCorps Members: 115
Description: AmeriCorps Members will improve the academic achievement of K-12 youth through coordinating service learning projects through a school-based watershed restoration curriculum. AmeriCorps Members will also serve as mentors and work in crews to restore watersheds by building trails and planting trees.
Contact: Kim Stokley; 919/628-5334; 916/628-4212 (fax)

CA-36

Los Angeles:
Program: Building Up Los Angeles
AmeriCorps Members: 152
Description: AmeriCorps Members will participate in a strong city-wide collaboration of over sixty organizations coming together to serve Los Angeles neighborhoods. Each neighborhood has a mix of projects tailored to the needs of the individual area, but will focus on children, youth, and families. The approach will be multi-service, comprehensive, and build local capacity to continue the programs after the funding has stopped.
Contact: Kristen Haggins; 213/389-8580; 213/389-9712

CA-37

Los Angeles:
Program: Building Up Los Angeles/Cluster Development Proposal
AmeriCorps Members:
Description: This plan will extend the Building Up Los Angeles program to the San Fernando Valley.
Contact: Cathie Mostovoy; 213-749-3031; 213/749-0409 (fax)

CA-38

Los Angeles:
Program: Los Angeles Unified School District/LAUSD AmeriCorps Campus Safety Aides Initiative
AmeriCorps Members: 80
Description: AmeriCorps Members will pro-

mote public safety in 16 target elementary schools throughout Los Angeles. They will provide campus supervision, establish safe corridors, work with new and existing neighborhood watch groups, and provide emergency preparedness training for students.
Contact: Buren Simmons; 213/625-6440; 213/625-4574 (fax)

CA-39

Oakland:
Program: East Bay Conservation Corps/East Bay Conservation Corps AmeriCorps Collaborative
AmeriCorps Members: 140
Description: AmeriCorps Members will tutor and counsel at-risk youth, develop and operate after-school programs, deliver basic health care services, and implement physical improvement projects through a 19 organization partnership.
Contact: Ms. Joanna Lennon; 510/891-3900; 510/272-9001 (fax)

CA-40

Pomona:
Program: Cal Poly Pomona Foundation, Inc./PolyCorps-An AmeriCorps Project
AmeriCorps Members: 53
Description: AmeriCorps Members will form the PolyCorps to serve the community surrounding the CalPoly-Pomona campus. AmeriCorps Members will teach conflict resolution, coordinate community volunteers and community service projects in schools, and implement neighborhood physical improvement projects.
Contact: Polly Patterson; 909/869-2841; 909/869-4373 (fax)

CA-41

Richmond:
Program: Bay Area Community Resources/Bay Area Youth Agency Consortium AmeriCorps Project
AmeriCorps Members: 70
Description: AmeriCorps Members will meet the needs of at-risk youth through peer counseling, health education and outreach, gang intervention, conflict resolution, alcohol/drug counseling and education, outreach to homeless youth, after-school recreation,

tutoring, and child care.
Contact: Kim Smith; 415/362-4481; 415/362-4484 (fax)

CA-42

Sacramento:
Program: California Conservation Corps/A Cadre of Corps "Community Service Leaders"
AmeriCorps Members: 220
Description: AmeriCorps Members, as program leaders, will establish linkages between the California Conservation Corps and local communities. They will develop and implement mutually identified service projects including mentoring at-risk youth, and organizing community watches.
Contact: Deborah Nguyen; 916/324-4785; 445-1007 (fax)

CA-43

Sacramento:
Program: California Conservation Corps/CCC-AmeriCorps
AmeriCorps Members: 57
Description: AmeriCorps Members will work on diverse projects at three sites with activities ranging from environmental conservation work such as erosion control, park beautification, and wildlife preservation to human needs activities such as conflict resolution and anti-substance abuse workshops.
Contact: Deborah Nguyen, Madeline Lynn; 916/324-4785; 445-1007 (fax) Lake Tahoe: Bill Martinez, Jim Teagarten; 916/577-1061; 916/577-4932 (fax); Salinas: Brenda Herrmann; 408/475-1131; 408/475-8350 (fax); Anaheim: Carol Cooley; 714/776-2677; 714/776-2752 (fax)

CA-44

San Diego:
Program: San Diego Consortium & Private Industry Council/Safe Zones for Learning Americorps Partnership
AmeriCorps Members: 28
Description: AmeriCorps Members will address the safety and welfare of youth and families in Mid-City San Diego. Teams will organize citizen safety patrols in schools; provide multi-lingual parent outreach; offer pregnancy and dropout prevention counsel-

ing; and coordinate comprehensive health screenings to pre-school children.
Contact: Mr. Robert Lewison, Olivia Heth; 619/238-1445; 619/238-6063 (fax)

CA-45

San Diego:
Program: San Diego State University Foundation/California YMCA PRYDE AmeriCorps
AmeriCorps Members: 50
Description: AmeriCorps Members will provide youths with alternatives to juvenile crime and delinquency by expanding after-school programs, providing one-on-one mentoring, enhancing parental and family involvement, coordinating community service projects, and delivering substance abuse awareness workshops.
Contact: John Wedemeyer, Robin King; 619/594-4756; 619/287-6756 (fax)

CA-46

San Diego:
Program: The Urban Corps of San Diego/A San Diego Safety Partnership: The Balboa Park Ranger Corps
AmeriCorps Members: 20
Description: AmeriCorps Members will reduce crime and increase park use by forming the Balboa Park Ranger Corps to conduct safety patrols in conjunction with the San Diego Police Department.
Contact: Sam Lopez; 619/235-0137; 619/232-7467 (fax)

CA-47

San Francisco:
Program: California Court Appointed Special Advocate Assoc./California CASA Programs
AmeriCorps Members: 25
Description: AmeriCorps Members will advocate for at-risk and abused children in the juvenile justice system; increase community awareness of child abuse issues; encourage a home atmosphere where education is valued; and recruit, screen, train, and supervise volunteers to serve as mentors for abused children.
Contact: Christine Mayer; 415/546-7365; 415/546-6598 (fax)

CA-48

San Francisco:
Program: Volunteer Center of San Francisco/Linking San Francisco
AmeriCorps Members: 20
Description: AmeriCorps Members will work in ten schools to offer service-learning experiences for students and provide them with leadership opportunities through youth advisory councils, peer tutoring, and conflict mediation.
Contact: Tajel Shah; 415/759-2882; 415/759-2903 (fax)

CA-49

San Francisco:
Program: Partners In School Innovation/The Tides Foundation
AmeriCorps Members: 13
Description: AmeriCorps Members will make service-learning a tool for educational reform in 4 public schools in low-income areas. Members will enhance academic achievement by developing educational service projects, parent-participation programs, and youth leadership opportunities.
Contact: Ms. Kim Grose; 415/824-6196; 415/824-6198 (fax)

CA-50

Santa Ana:
Program: Building Community
AmeriCorps Members: 22
Description: AmeriCorps Members will be placed at four public housing centers to deliver multi-services, including providing child care to residents, working with residents to identify needs and enable them with the resources needed to overcome those needs. In addition, members will conduct community based research and evaluation of the planning process at each child care center.
Contact: Helen Brown, Lydia Casamina; 714/835-0406; 714/835-7354 (fax)

CA-51

Santa Rosa:
Program: Sonoma County Community Service Coalition/The Sonoma Project
AmeriCorps Members: 21

Description: AmeriCorps Members will develop "safe-haven" after-school centers, provide in-home support services for formerly homeless youth, and engage in gang prevention activities.

Contact: Johnetta Dedrick; 707/544-6911; 707/526-2918 (fax)

State Priorities:

Education

1. Place adult and youth role models in mentoring and tutorial relationships with students who are at risk of dropping out of school or academic failure, including teen parents who receive Aid to Families with Dependent Children.

2. Provide service participants skills and experiences that will lead to gainful employment or additional community service opportunities.

3. Improve the readiness of all students to learn the district's core curriculum and progress as rapidly as they are able.

4. Provide service experiences that improve the willingness to work, sense of personal and social efficacy, and academic achievement of all students, regardless of their background, and particularly the disadvantaged, limited English speaking, disabled and other students who are at risk of failure in school.

Public Safety

1. Reduce juvenile crime.

2. Assure that all school campuses will be areas of absolute safety.

Human Needs

1. Encourage preventive approaches to meeting unmet human needs.

2. Assist economically depressed areas of the State.

3. Reduce the social fragmentation of our communities by identifying common areas of interest in which people from different backgrounds can work together, achieve results, and build trust.

4. Reconnect parents and children to their schools and communities.

5. Improve the health of children, their families and communities.

Environment

1. Assist communities affected by natural disasters.

2. Improve the aesthetic, safety, and historical aspects of the local environment.

COLORADO

State Lead Contact:

John Calhoon
Office of the Governor
136 State Capitol Building
Denver, CO 80203
Phone: 303/866-2120
Fax: 303/866-2003

1995-96 Programs

National Service Network

CO-1

Statewide:
Program: USDA Rural Development Teach
AmeriCorps Members: 50 (Four Corners)
Description: AmeriCorps Members will help communities protect watersheds, improve housing, promote economic development, boost sustainable agriculture and respond to disasters.
Contact: Joel Berg; 202/720-6350

CO-2

Colorado Springs:
Program: Youth Volunteer Corps of America/Leadership Corps
AmeriCorps Members: 8 (107 Nationally)
Description: AmeriCorps Members will develop, run, and enroll volunteers in service projects including: summer camps, academic enrichment programs, service-learning curricula, conflict resolution training, gang alternative programs, and identification of high crime areas.
Contact: David Battey; 913/432-9822

CO-3

Denver:
Program: Council of Great City Schools
AmeriCorps Members: To Be Determined
Description: AmeriCorps Members will
recruit teachers, develop service-learning
programs, organize model service corps of
volunteers working as school/classroom
aides, literacy tutors, and academic mentors.
Contact: Michael Casserly; 202/393-2427

State and Local

CO-4

Denver:
Program: Office of Rural Job Training/Col-
orado HIPPY AmeriCorps
AmeriCorps Members: 16
Description: AmeriCorps Members will provide home-based and peer-delivered training
in family literacy, parenting skills, and pre-
school readiness to 180 poor and under-edu-
cated parents of three- and four-year-old
children in four Empowerment/Enterprise
Zones in urban and rural Colorado
Contact: J. Dwight Steele; 303/894-7410;
303/894-7416 (fax)

CO-5

Denver:
Program: Cole Coalition, Inc./Cole: Building Community
AmeriCorps Members: 24
Description: AmeriCorps Members will
reduce high crime rates and rehabilitate distressed properties by renovating boarded and
vacant houses for low-income families, rehabilitating vacant lots for community use,
improving child care services, and providing
life-skills education for Cole residents.
Contact: Ms. Barbara Semien; 303/293-
2188; 303/298-8023 (fax)

CO-6

Denver:
Program: Volunteers of America Colorado
Branch, Inc./Metro Denver Gang Prevention
Program
AmeriCorps Members: 20
Description: AmeriCorps Members will
reduce gang activity and teen violence by
serving in 13 Metro Denver Gang Coalition

agencies as block organizers, volunteer coordinators, parent educators, drug prevention
counselors, tutors and mentors, community
liaisons, volunteer coordinators, and peer
counselors.
Contact: Ms. Dianna Kunz; 303/297-0408;
303/297-2310 (fax)

CO-7

Englewood:
Program: Sheridan School District #26/
Sheridan Family Resource Center Project
AmeriCorps Members: 22
Description: AmeriCorps Members will
improve health care in a medically under-
served area by creating and staffing the
Sheridan Family Resource Center and by
providing a broad range of services including
health care, child care, social services, mental health services, education, recreation, and
senior services.
Contact: Ms. Sharon Coleman; 303/761-
6375; 303/789-2611 (fax)

CO-8

Glenwood Springs:
Program: Colorado Mountain College/Com-
munity Collaboration Team
AmeriCorps Members: 20
Description: AmeriCorps members will
respond to needs arising from the rapid
growth of an "underclass" in the rural resort
region of Colorado by developing a network
system among service providers and establishing a case management system of at-risk
families and youth in order to prevent substance abuse and crimes.
Contact: Ms. Mariana Velasquez-Schmahl

CONNECTICUT

State Lead Contact:

Nancy Mandell
CT Department of Higher Education
61 Woodland Street
Hartford, CT 06105
Phone: 203/566-6154
Fax: 203/566-7865

1995-96 Programs

National Service Network

CT-1

Bridgeport:
Program: ASPIRA Association, Inc.
AmeriCorps Members: 13 (40 Nationally)
Description: AmeriCorps Members will establish a holistic service-delivery model for assisting Latino students and parents with language, literacy, and math skills. AmeriCorps Members will also train youth in conflict resolution and violence prevention.
Contact: Ronald Blackburn-Moreno; 202/835-3600

CT-2

Hartford:
Program: I Have a Dream Foundation/AmeriCorps Partnership
AmeriCorps Members: 7 (114 Nationally)
Description: Members will mentor and tutor student "Dreamers" from disadvantaged areas, giving personal guidance to reduce the dropout rate, increase parental and community involvement in the schools, and to develop service opportunities.
Contact: Daniel Moralies; 201/275-8281

CT-3

New Haven:
Program: Green Corps' Neighborhood Green Corps Program
AmeriCorps Members: 5 (60 Nationally)
Description: Splitting their time between projects involving the home environment and the community environment, AmeriCorps Members will educate and then activate their communities through three projects: low income home weatherization, lead paint abatement, and urban gardening.
Contact: Ms. Leslie Samuelrich; 617/426-8506

CT-4

New Haven:
Program: I Have a Dream Foundation/AmeriCorps Partnership
AmeriCorps Members: 8 (114 Nationally)
Description: Members will mentor and tutor student "Dreamers" from disadvantaged

areas, giving personal guidance to prevent dropouts.
Contact: Rebecca West; 203/436-3556

CT-5

Hartford:
Program: Local Initiatives Support Corporation
AmeriCorps Members:
Description: Call contact for information.
Contact: Elizabeth Swanzy -Parker; 203/525-4821; 203/525-4822 (fax)

CT-6

New Haven:
Program: Summerbridge AmeriCorps Teaching Program
AmeriCorps Members: 68 Nationally
Description: AmeriCorps Members will recruit high school and college students to teach disadvantaged middle school students. The objective will be to improve their academic and leadership performance.
Contact: Ms. Catina Bacote; 203/397-1001; 203/389-2249 (fax)

CT-7

Hartford:
Program: US Catholic Conference
AmeriCorps Members:
Description: Call contact for information.
Contact: Stephanie Morton; Jim Cole; 203/548-0049; 203/543-7151 (fax)

State and Local

CT-8

Bridgeport:
Program: Volunteer Center of Greater Bridgeport/Bridgeport Inter Regional AmeriCorps Program
AmeriCorps Members: 49
Description: AmeriCorps Members will be placed at 23 host sites in 3 regions where they will manage community volunteers who will construct low-income houses, tutor adult learners, provide health information and referral, and perform chores for the elderly.
Contact: Ms. Carol Elliott; 203/266-9466; 203/334-3297 (fax)

CT-9

Hartford:
Program: City of Hartford/Hartford Ameri-
Corps
AmeriCorps Members:
Description: Planning grant to develop a
youth corps program based on the City Year
model. The planning period will solidify program objectives to meet local needs, design
effective service activities, develop training
workshops, and locate service sites.
Contact: Robert Rath; 203/296-5068

CT-10

New Haven:
Program: Leadership, Education and Athletics in Partnership/Leadership, Education
and Athletics in Partnership
AmeriCorps Members: 164
Description: AmeriCorps Members forming
a diverse corps of college and high school
students will provide academic skills building, mentoring, and community support to
696 inner-city children. During summer
months participants will live in public housing where the children they assist reside.
Contact: Mr. Henry Fernandez; 203/773-
0770; 203/773-1695 (fax)

CT-11

Bridgeport:
Program: Youth in Service Ambassadors
AmeriCorps
AmeriCorps Members: 9 full- and 57 part-
time
Description: AmeriCorps Members will
work to reduce crime, violence, and fear in
targeted neighborhoods.
Contact: Muata Langley; 203/335-8835

CT-12

Meriden:
Program: CitySERVE!
AmeriCorps Members: 18
Description: AmeriCorps Members will
work to improve school readiness skills in
preschool and school-aged children and
parenting skills in young parents.
Contact: Karyn Krystock; 203/630-4208

CT-13

Greater Middlesex County:
Program: CAGMC
AmeriCorps Members: 33
Description: AmeriCorps Members will
work in the areas of human service, educa-
tion, and public and youth safety.
Contact: Betty A. Walsh; 203/347-4465

DELAWARE

State Lead Contact:

Anne Farley
DHSS Herman M. Holloway Campus
1901 N. DuPont Hwy., bldg. T
New Castle, DE 19720
Phone: 302/577-4961
Fax: 302/577-4975

1995-96 Programs

State and Local

DE-1

Dover:
Program: Dover Housing Authority/Dover
Community Service Challenge
AmeriCorps Members: 20
Description: AmeriCorps Members will
improve the quality of life in four public
housing communities by helping residents
access health services, developing home
ownership opportunities, and implementing
a drug and crime prevention program to
strengthen neighborhood security.
Contact: Ms. Denise Schott; 302/678-1965;
302/678-1971 (fax)

DE-2

Wilmington:
Program: National Multiple Sclerosis Soci-
ety/ "Bridge to Independence"
AmeriCorps Members: 8 (144 Nationally)
Description: AmeriCorps Members, many of
whom have Multiple Sclerosis, will work to
build awareness about Multiple Sclerosis
while coordinating volunteers in extensive
living assistance programs—helping disadvantaged people to make it on their own.
Contact: Marilyn Van Savage; 302/655-
5610; 302/655-0993 (fax)

DISTRICT OF COLUMBIA

State Lead Contact:

Ms. Ressie Walker
DC Office of Policy
717 14th Street, NW, #900
Washington DC 20004
Phone: 202/727-6979
Fax: 202/727-3333

1995-96 Programs

National Service Network

DC-1

Program: DC Habitat for Humanity
AmeriCorps Members: To be determined
Description: AmeriCorps Members will
work in the area of housing. Call contact for
information.
Contact: Carol Casperson; 202/563-3411;
202/562-4336 (fax)

DC-2

Program: Local Initiatives Support Corpora-
tion/LISC AmeriCorps
AmeriCorps Members: To be determined
Description: AmeriCorps Members will
work in the area of environment/human
needs. Call contact for information.
Contact: Susie Sinclair-Smith; 202/785-
2908; 202/835-8931 (fax)

DC-3

Program: U.S. Department of Energy
AmeriCorps Members: To be determined
Description: AmeriCorps Members will
work in the area of environment. Call contact
for information.
Contact: Robert Nixon; 202/889-2020; 202/
889-0029 (fax)

DC-4

Program: Green Corps' Neighborhood
Green Corps Program
AmeriCorps Members: 5 (60 Nationally)
Description: Splitting their time between
projects involving the home environment
and the community environment, Ameri-
Corps Members will educate and then acti-

vate their communities through three
projects: low income home weatherization,
lead paint abatement, and urban gardening.
Contact: Ms. Leslie Samuelrich; 617/426-
8506

DC-5

Program: Public Allies
AmeriCorps Members: To be determined
Description: AmeriCorps Members will
work in the areas of education and public
safety.
Contact: Becky Duffy; 202/638-3300; 202/
638-3477 (fax)

DC-6

Program: I Have a Dream Foundation/Ame-
riCorps Partnership
AmeriCorps Members: 14 (114 Nationally)
Description: Members will mentor and tutor
student "Dreamers" from disadvantaged
areas, giving personal guidance to prevent
dropouts.
Contact: Gregg Brown; 202/628-2951

DC-7

Program: Mid-Atlantic Network of Youth
and Family Services/MANY Youth and
Community Development Corps
AmeriCorps Members: 15
Description: AmeriCorps Members will
facilitate a runaway and homeless youth service project aimed at leadership development
through community service. This program
will meet the dual needs of community assistance and self-esteem building for the youth
it involves.
Contact: Lori Kaplan, Latin American
Youth Center; 202/483-1140

DC-8

Program: National Endowment for the Arts/
The Writers Corps
AmeriCorps Members: 20
Description: AmeriCorps Members will
work with homeless and runaway youth in
creative writing and poetry workshops in
order to improve writing and verbal skills,
while boosting self-worth.
Contact: William Aguado; 718/931-9500

DC-9

Program: The Neighborhood Reinvestment Corporation
AmeriCorps Members: 30 Nationally
Description: The NeighborWorks Community Corps, with which AmeriCorps Members will work, promotes neighborhood stabilization through home ownership and crime prevention. AmeriCorps Members will assist with mortgage financing, work to establish Neighborhood Watch groups, and organize community rehabilitation in needy cities throughout the country.
Contact: Ronald L. Walker; 202/376-3216

DC-10

Program: Teach for America
AmeriCorps Members: 65 (1000 Nationally)
Description: AmeriCorps Members will respond to an acute need for educators and role models in under-served urban and rural areas by introducing innovative teaching methods to the classroom.
Contact: Wendy Kopp; 212/432-1272

State and Local

DC-11

Washington:
Program: Latin American Youth Center/ Multicultural Urban Health Corps
AmeriCorps Members: To be determined
Description: AmeriCorps Members will work in the area of education. Call contact for information.
Contact: Monique Turner; 202/483-1140; 202/462-5696 (fax)

FLORIDA

State Lead Contact:

Dr. Chris Gilmore, Executive Director
Tabatha Burn McMahon, Programs Director
1101 Gulf Breeze Parkway
Suite 331
Gulf Breeze, FL 32561
Phone: 904/934-4000
Fax: 904/934-4006

Additional State Contact:

Joe Martin

State Commission:

Governor's Commission on Community Service and Public/Private Partnerships

1995-96 Programs

National Service Network

FL-1

Statewide:
(Rural areas)
Program: HHS - Head Start/Family Serve
AmeriCorps Members: 15
Description: For the children of migrant farmworker communities, AmeriCorps Members will provide literacy tutoring, and their parents will be educated in basic parenting skills to help improve school success. Families will also receive needed health and social services project.
Contact: JoEllen Shannon; 703/243-7522; Tom Logan; 813/299-7484

FL-2

Clearwater:
Program: Neighborworks Community Corps—Neighborhood Housing Services, Inc.
AmeriCorps Members: 2
Description: Two members based with Clearwater NHS, Inc., to focus on commercial loan development and organizing merchants to address a youth gang issue, and to focus on block organizing for crime prevention.
Contact: Marcella Williams; 202/376-3214; Nancy Hansen; 813/442-4155

FL-3

Everglades:
Program: Department of the Interior/Everglades South Florida Ecosystem
AmeriCorps Members: 110 (505 Nationally)
Description: Charged with protecting the delicate Everglades ecosystem, AmeriCorps Members will work with specialists in monitoring plant and animal life in addition to doing restoration projects and providing environmental education.

Contact: Richard Ring; 305/242-7700; Larry Belli or Jim Brown; 305/242-7770

FL-4

Everglades:
Program: Department of the Interior/Earth Science Field Corps
AmeriCorps Members: 125 (505 Nationally)
Description: AmeriCorps Members will work with the US Geological Survey to enhance federal and state environmental studies including computer science, cartography, statistics, and surveying.
Contact: Sue Keminitzer; 202/208-4009

FL-5

Homestead:
Program: Habitat for Humanity International
AmeriCorps Members: 47
Description: AmeriCorps Members will help build 200 homes in the new, environmentally sensitive Jordan Commons development.
Contact: David McDaniels; 912/924-6935, ext. 193; Dorothy Adair or Rick Barry; 305/247-0847

FL-6

Jacksonville:
Program: YMCA Earth Service Corps Fellowship
AmeriCorps Members: 40 Nationally
Description: AmeriCorps Members will address local environmental concerns, coordinating park cleanups, urban gardening projects, and environmental symposia.
Contact: Celeste Wroblewski; 312/269-0506; Ann West; 904/272-4304, ext. 23

FL-7

Miami:
Program: Children's Health Fund/AmeriCorps Community Outreach
AmeriCorps Members: 4 (15 Nationally)
Description: The Children's Health Fund was designed to meet the complex health care needs of medically under-served, homeless, and impoverished children. AmeriCorps Members will work to this end by encouraging families to take advantage of available primary health care resources.
Contact: Linda Anderson; 304/525-3334;

Gwen Wurm, M.D., or Elena Urbye; 305/547-3818

FL-8

Miami:
Program: Habitat for Humanity International
AmeriCorps Members: 48
Description: AmeriCorps Members will work on the construction of 90 houses for low-income families who were victims of Hurricane Andrew.
Contact: David McDaniels; 912/924-6935, ext. 193; Ian Stuart or Kevin McPeak; 305/670-2224

FL-9

Miami
Program: Summerbridge AmeriCorps Teaching Program
AmeriCorps Members: 68 Nationally
Description: AmeriCorps Members will recruit high school and college students to teach disadvantaged middle school students. The objective will be to improve their academic and leadership performance.
Contact: Lois Loofbourrow; 415/749-2037; John Flickinger; 305/443-0735

FL-10

Vero Beach:
Program: Youth Volunteer Corps of America/YVCA Leadership Corps
AmeriCorps Members: 6 (107 Nationally)
Description: AmeriCorps Members will develop, run, and enroll volunteers in service projects including: summer camps, academic enrichment programs, service-learning curricula, conflict resolution training, gang alternative programs, and identification of high crime areas.
Contact: David Battey; 913/432-9822; Diane Hunkle; 407/562-9036

State and Local

FL-11

Brooksville:
Program: City of Brooksville/AmeriCorps Hernando
AmeriCorps Members: 14
Description: AmeriCorps Members,

recruited mainly from the areas being served, will organize literacy programs; establish crime watch programs; create neighborhood clean-up projects; and help restructure local social services.
Contact: Mr. Ray Schumaker; 904/544-5430; 904/544-5424 (fax); Frank Godfrey; 904/544-5406

FL-12

Fort Lauderdale:
Program: Broward County Sheriff's Office/ AmeriCorps Broward-Coalition for Community Empowerment
AmeriCorps Members: 40
Description: AmeriCorps Members will work in three high-poverty, high-crime, inner-city neighborhoods to establish after-school programs, assist victims of crime, provide youth alternatives to drug activities, conduct seminars on discipline strategies, and restore deteriorated recreation facilities.
Contact: Mr. Steve Sampier; 305/831-8901; 305/797-0936 (fax); Helene Tragus; 305/ 831-8935

FL-13

Fort Meyers:
Program: The Coalition for a Drug Free Lee County/Fort Meyers/Lee County Ameri-Corps Program
AmeriCorps Members: 15
Description: AmeriCorps Members will provide mentoring, vocational training, tutorial services, substance abuse treatment programs, volunteer community patrols, and child care services to create a safe and productive environment for families in a targeted area of Fort Meyers.
Contact: Mr. David Graham; 813/443-4380; 813/433-4380 (fax); Mike Carr; 813/338-2223

FL-14

Frostproof:
Program: Frostproof Care Center, Inc./AmeriCorps Frostproof
AmeriCorps Members: 20
Description: AmeriCorps Members will provide tutoring, study skills, training on recognizing and avoiding crime and education on nutrition and substance abuse prevention in a

collaborative community-based effort to meet the needs of a rural area.
Contact: Mr. Ralph Waters; 813/635-5555; 813/635-9202 (fax); Ben Newcomer; 813/ 635-2551

FL-15

Jacksonville:
Program: Neighborhood Economic Development Initiative/AmeriCorps Jacksonville Coalition Grant Proposal
AmeriCorps Members: 12 full-time; 16 part-time
Description: AmeriCorps Members will work to break generational cycles of dependency, decrease youth violence, and foster neighbor interaction by tutoring, mentoring, boarding up abandoned buildings, creating community gardens, and providing child abuse and crisis prevention services.
Contact: Mr. Gregory Owens; 904/630-1905; 904/630-1485 (fax); Kathy Wolff; 904/630-2966

FL-16

Miami:
Program: AmeriCorps Dade
AmeriCorps Members: 60
Description: AmeriCorps Members will work in collaboration with 28 agencies in Florida's largest program to decrease neighborhood disorder and decline in five neighborhoods by establishing crime watch programs, conducting conflict resolution seminars and rehabilitating abandoned buildings.
Contact: Mr. Harve Mogul; 305/579-2215; 305/579-2225 (fax); Emme Dedinelli; (305) 579-2282

FL-17

Pensacola:
Program: Escambia-Pensacola Human Relations Commission/AmeriCorps Escambia County—The Engelwood Initiative
AmeriCorps Members: 15
Description: AmeriCorps members will establish a target hardening program, implement crime watches, improve street lighting, build a community park and create three new businesses in order to lower the rate of neighborhood crime, increase economic

development and rehabilitate abandoned buildings.

Contact: Mr. Eugene Brown; 904/434-2431; 904/434-9914 (fax); Grover Brown; 904/434-2431

FL-18

St. Petersburg:
Program: St. Petersburg Junior College—Criminal Justice Institute/AmeriCorps Pinellas County
AmeriCorps Members: 11
Description: AmeriCorps Members will support community policing officers in mobilizing community involvement in crime prevention, victim assistance activities and neighborhood beautification projects; tutor prison inmates; and conduct home security surveys, all while obtaining a degree in Criminal Justice. (This is part of the program described below.)
Contact: Ms. Kathleen Corr; 813/341-4502; 813/341-4547 (fax); Eileen LaHie; 813/341-4493

FL-19

St. Petersburg:
Program: St. Petersburg Junior College—Criminal Justice Institute/AmeriCorps Pinellas County
AmeriCorps Members: 29
Description: AmeriCorps Members will support community policing officers in mobilizing community involvement in crime prevention, victim assistance activities and neighborhood beautification projects; tutor prison inmates; and conduct home security surveys, all while obtaining a degree in Criminal Justice. (This is part of the program described above.)
Contact: Ms. Kathleen Corr; 813/341-4502; 813/341-4547 (fax); Eileen LaHie; 813/341-4493

FL-20

Stuart:
Program: United Way of Martin County/AmeriCorps Martin County
AmeriCorps Members: 15
Description: AmeriCorps Members will work in three underserved communities in Martin County to enable residents to move towards self-sufficiency by offering tutoring, revitalizing public housing, conducting home security assessments, increasing recreational activities and providing prenatal care.
Contact: Mr. Harry Yates; 407/288-5758; 407/288-5799 (fax); Lindy Rich; 407/287-7702

FL-21

Tavares:
Program: Lake County Board of County Commissioners/UNITY—AmeriCorps Lake County
AmeriCorps Members: 10 full-time; 6 part-time
Description: AmeriCorps Members, as part of a community resident generated collaboration, will work with residents to provide educational and tutoring services; assist the elderly and homebound; rehabilitate houses; and create community patrols and a Neighborhood Watch program.
Contact: Ms. Myra Smith; 904/343-9430; 904/343-9896 (fax); Fletcher Smith; 904/343-9630

State Priorities:

Commission Rankings of Issues and Priorities (2/2/3/94)

Issues:

(1) Human Needs; (2) Education; (3) Public Safety; (4) Environment; Other: Employment

Comments: Public safety needs to be a part of education.

Priorities:

HUMAN NEEDS

(1) Home; (2) Health; (3) Employment; (4) Other: Substance abuse prevention

Comments: Under Health, community support for frail elders to stay in-home

EDUCATION

(1) School Readiness; (2) School Success; (3) Adult Literacy; (4) Other: Tied between Self/Esteem/Life Skills Education and Service Learning on all levels

PUBLIC SAFETY

(1) Crime Prevention; (2) Crime Control; (3)Other: Employment Development

ENVIRONMENT

(1) Neighborhood Environment; (2) Natural Environment

GEORGIA

State Lead Contact:

Lynn Thornton, Executive Director
2020 Equitable Building
100 Peachtree Street
Atlanta, GA 30303
Phone: 404/657-7827
Fax: 404/657-7835

State Commission:

Georgia Commission for National and Community Service

1995-96 Programs

National Service Network

GA-1

Statewide:
Program: HHS—Administration on Developmental Disabilities
AmeriCorps Members: 70 Nationally
Description: AmeriCorps Members will provide personal assistance services to increase the social and economic independence of individuals with developmental disabilities.
Contact: Jeanette Senarr; 770/531-6461

GA-2

Statewide:
Program: National Multiple Sclerosis Society/ "Bridge to Independence"
AmeriCorps Members: 8 (144 Nationally)
Description: AmeriCorps Members, many of whom have Multiple Sclerosis, will work to build awareness about Multiple Sclerosis while coordinating volunteers in extensive living assistance programs—helping disadvantaged people to make it on their own.
Contact: Connie Divine; 770/984-9080; 770//984-9352 (fax)

GA-3

Atlanta:
Program: Family Literacy Corps
Description: AmeriCorps Members will teach adults and children how to read.
Contact: Sandra Moore; 404/756-3835

GA-4

Americus:
Program: Habitat for Humanity International
AmeriCorps Members: 35
Description: AmeriCorps Members will build 60 houses in the county-wide effort involving civic groups, churches, and businesses.
Contact: Heather Erickson; 912/924-6935, ext. 134

GA-5

Atlanta:
Program: Greater Atlanta Community Corps
Description: AmeriCorps Members will take part in neighborhood revitalization and environmental protection projects.
Contact: J. D. Ferguson; 404/522-4322

GA-6

Atlanta:
Program: "Safety Net—A Campaign Against Violence"
AmeriCorps Members: 10
Description: A broad coalition of colleges will support this AmeriCorps program designed to curb violence through counseling, training, and the development of solutions. In Atlanta, for instance, AmeriCorps Members will assist groups in building rope courses used to train middle school students in peer mediation and conflict resolution.
Contact: Kweko Forstall; 404/215-2724

GA-7

Atlanta:
Program: Public Education Fund Network/ Project FIRST (Fostering Instructional Reform Through Service and Technology)
AmeriCorps Members: 11
Description: Working with retired technology experts, AmeriCorps Members will integrate new educational technologies into

instruction across subject areas, increasing student access by 20 percent.
Contact: Nancy Hamilton; 404/249-7763

GA-8

Atlanta:
Program: USDA Public Lands and Environment Team
AmeriCorps Members: 20 (564 Nationally)
Description: As part of a national effort to restore public lands and reduce community environmental hazards, AmeriCorps Members will monitor and rehabilitate five impaired streams in the Atlanta metropolitan area.
Contact: Cindy Haygood; 770/528-2218

GA-9

Waycross:
Program: National Association of Child Care Resources and Referral Agencies
Description: AmeriCorps Members will serve in and assist child care agencies.
Contact: Yvonne Jeffords; 912/264-0035

GA-10

Atlanta:
Program: YouthBuild USA, Inc.
Description: AmeriCorps Members teach construction skills to at-risk youth.
Contact: Susan Everett; 770/493-4443

State and Local

GA-11

Thomson:
Program: Georgia Peach/AmeriCorps
Description: AmeriCorps Members will participate in tutoring, mentoring, senior citizen visitation, and environmental revitalization.
Contact: David Moore; 706/595-2185

GA-12

Atlanta:
Program: Metro Atlanta Task Force for the Homeless/Task Force Service Corps
AmeriCorps Members: 20
Description: AmeriCorps Members will help homeless families become self-sufficient by providing assistance finding shelter, offering employment counseling, and providing tutoring to homeless families.

Contact: Atiba Mbiwan; 404/230-5000; 404/489-8251 (fax)

GA-13

Atlanta:
Program: Hands On Atlanta, Inc./Hands On Atlanta Youth Corps
AmeriCorps Members: 65
Description: AmeriCorps Members will work in area elementary schools as teaching assistants, tutors, mentors and role models. In conjunction with adult volunteers, AmeriCorps members will also develop and lead projects to renovate community centers, beautify parks, and upgrade housing projects.
Contact: Mr. Ron Riggs; 404/872-2252; 404/872-2251 (fax)

GA-14

Decatur:
Program: Georgia School-Age Care Association, Inc./The 3:00 Project
AmeriCorps Members: 19
Description: AmeriCorps Members will create three new after-school programs at area middle-schools where Members will tutor, involve students in community service, and lead team building and motivation exercises.
Contact: Dr. Mercedes Smith; 404/373-7414; 404/373-7428 (fax)

GA-15

Decatur:
Program: Macon Police AmeriCorps Cadets
Description: AmeriCorps Members will participate in public safety and community policing activities.
Contact: James May; 912/751-7510

GA-16

Douglas:
Program: City of Douglas: Douglas/Coffee County Service Corps
AmeriCorps Members: 20
Description: AmeriCorps Members will help create a new emergency 911 network, renovate parks, plant trees and grass, offer adult literacy tutoring, and serve as translators in court.
Contact: Ms. Ivey Kight; 912/384-4841; 912/384-0291 (fax)

GA-17

Macon:
Program: Mid State Children's Challenge Projects Inc./Georgia Challenge Corps
AmeriCorps Members: 30
Description: AmeriCorps Members will create an arts-based after-school and summer camp program to bring together children with and without disabilities. AmeriCorps members will also help create the Center for Independent Living in middle Georgia by renovating dwellings and making home visits.
Contact: Dr. Thomas Glennon; 912/752-2952 or 912/745-3760; 912/752-4124 (fax)

GA-18

Albany:
Program: After School AmeriCorps
Description: AmeriCorps Members will take part in programs for children with disabilities.
Contact: Beth English; 912/439-7062

GA-19

LaGrange:
Program: Care Link AmeriCorps
Description: AmeriCorps Members will provide in-home services for the elderly and disabled.
Contact: Ms. Edna DeGennaro; 706/845-3723

GA-20

Atlanta:
Program: YMCA: Academic Enhancement AmeriCorps
Description: AmeriCorps Members will work in tutoring and English as a Second Language programs for elementary students

State Priorities:

Same as national priorities

HAWAI'I

State Lead Contact:

Mr. John Sabas
Hawai'i Commission for National and Community Service
335 Merchant Street, Room 101

Honolulu, HI 96813
Phone: 808/586-8675
Fax: 808/586-8685

State Commission:

Hawai'i Commission for National and Community Service

1995-96 Programs

State and Local

HI-1

O'ahu, Maui, Kaua'i counties, Hawai'i:
Program: Hawai'i Lawyers Care/Student Advocacy for Victims of Domestic Violence
AmeriCorps Members: 40
Description: AmeriCorps members, who are lawyers and legal advocate students, will assist domestic violence victims by serving as courthouse advocates in clinics at family courts throughout the state and by offering legal assistance at shelters and other family crisis centers.
Contact: Ms. Judy Sobin; 808/528-7051; 808/524-2147 (fax)

HI-2

Pahala:
Program: Institute for a Sustainable Future, Inc./Big Island AmeriCorps: Community Based Environmental Recovery
AmeriCorps Members: 20
Description: AmeriCorps members, including displaced sugar cane workers, will address local food, fuel, and reforestation needs by installing solar collectors, setting up fish breeding ponds, and tending native and medicinal tree seedlings.
Contact: Ms. Mary Ruchinskas; 808/928-6203; 808/928-9412 (fax)

State Priorities:

National priorities plus strengthening families.

IDAHO

State Lead Contact:

Kelly Houston
Idaho Commission for National and

Community Service
P.O. Box 83702
Boise, ID 83720
Phone: 208/334-3843
Fax: 208/334-2632

1995-96 Programs

National Service Network

ID-1

Columbia River Basin:
Program: United States Department of
Energy—Salmon Corps
AmeriCorps Members: 24
Description: AmeriCorps Participants, most
of whom will represent the 5 Native Ameri-
can tribes in the region, will work to restore
the critical salmon habitat of the Columbia
River Basin while restoring Native American
culture.
Contact: Howlie Davis; 202/586-7970

State and Local

ID-2

Boise:
Program: Idaho Department of Parks and
Recreation/Idaho AmeriCorps
AmeriCorps Members: 10
Description: AmeriCorps members will
coordinate service projects for 4th and 5th
graders in schools and for public park visi-
tors, plant vegetation on stream beds to promote erosion control, build nest boxes or
platforms for local wildlife, start school
recycling programs, and build trails with
informational signs.
Contract: Mr. William Dokken; 208/334-
4199; 208/334-3741 (fax)

ID-3

Lewiston:
Program: Lewis-Clark State College/Idaho
TRIO AmeriCorps Project
AmeriCorps Members: 26
Description: AmeriCorps Members will
work with a four college consortium to
establish tutor/mentor centers in schools that
will address low math/science skills; link
home and school through parenting classes;
deliver workshops on college preparation
and job search; and promote after-school

educational activities.
Contact: Dr. Mary Emery; 208/799-2460;
208/799-2878 (fax)

ILLINOIS

State Lead Contact:

Jeanne Bradner
Director of Commission Programs
Illinois Commission on Community Service
(ICCS)
Department of Commerce and Community
Affairs
100 W. Randolph St., Suite 3-400
Chicago, IL 60601
Phone: 312/814-5225; 800/592-9896
Fax: 312/814-7236

Additional Contact:

Mary Sleger, Director of Administration &
Finance

State Commission:

Illinois Commission on Community Service
(ICCS)

1995-96 Programs

National Service Network

IL-1

Statewide:
(Rural areas)
Program: Association of Farmworkers
Opportunity Program
AmeriCorps Members: 3 (61 Nationally)
Description: AmeriCorps Members will
train migrant and seasonal farmworkers on
how to reduce exposure to pesticides and
improve farmworkers' access to other health,
education and support services.
Contact: Lynda Mull; 703/528-4141

IL-2

Program: USDA Rural Development Team
AmeriCorps Members: 78 in the 9 Flood
States
Description: Responding to the environmental and economic damage caused by last
year's flood, AmeriCorps Members will
assess flood-relief needs, explain wetlands

delineation to land owners, and work to reduce ground water pollution.
Contact: Joel Berg; 202/720-6350

IL-3

Program: USDA Public Lands and Environment Team
AmeriCorps Members: 73 in the 9 Flood States
Description: AmeriCorps Members will engage a variety of flood relief work by assessing damage, restoring wetlands, and restoring flood control facilities.
Contact: Joel Berg; 202/720-6350

IL-4

Chicago:
Program: ACORN Housing Corporation
AmeriCorps Members: 42
Description: Working as intake and loan counselors, AmeriCorps Members will provide affordable housing opportunities for low and moderate-income families—a critical step in ACORN's community reinvestment program.
Contact: Michael Shea; 312/939-1611

IL-5

Chicago:
Program: City Year, Inc.
AmeriCorps Members: 55 (220 Nationally)
Description: Teams of AmeriCorps Members will comprehensively address interrelated community need.
Contact: Michael Brown/Alan Khazei; 617/451-0699

IL-6

Chicago:
Program: Department of Health & Human Services, Health Resources and Services Administration—"Model Health Service Corps"
AmeriCorps Members: 33 Nationally
Description: AmeriCorps Members will provide comprehensive community-based health care including home visits and outreach workshops.
Contact: John Westcott; 301/443-6880

IL-7

Chicago:
Program: I Have a Dream Foundation/AmeriCorps Partnership
AmeriCorps Members: 15 (114 Nationally)
Description: Members will mentor and tutor student "Dreamers" from disadvantaged areas, giving personal guidance to prevent dropouts.
Contact: John Horan; 312/787-8029

IL-8

Chicago:
Program: USDA Public Lands and Environment Team
AmeriCorps Members: 20
Description: AmeriCorps Members will recruit 500 volunteers to create sites that combine urban agriculture and public safety at public housing developments in addition to educating hundreds more about urban agriculture.
Contact: Joel Berg; 202/720-6350

IL-9

East St. Louis:
Program: USDA Public Lands and Environment Team
AmeriCorps Members: 20
Description: AmeriCorps Members will restore neglected lots, beautify green houses and restore several other urban environments.
Contact: Joel Berg; 202/720-6350

State and Local

IL-10

Chicago:
Program: Uptown Habitat for Humanity/Nobel Project National Service Program
AmeriCorps members: 15
Description: AmeriCorps members will rehabilitate low-income housing in the W. Humboldt Park neighborhood of Chicago where 33% of residents live in poverty. Some members will be recent high school graduates who are developing construction skills/career goals; others will support them with curriculum and career development.
Contact: Ms. Laura Leon; 312/252-8520; 312/252-8548 (fax)

IL-11

Chicago:

Program: Mid-America Chapter, American Red Cross/Americorps Health and Safety Services Program

AmeriCorps members: 22

Description: AmeriCorps Members will help underserved communities to provide health and safety education to diverse populations. Activities include recruiting volunteers and training them to provide safety, disaster, first aid, and HIV/AIDS education.

Contact: Ms. Susan Erickson; 312/440-2012; 312/527-1093 (fax)

IL-12

Chicago:

Program: Public Allies/Public Allies Chicago

AmeriCorps Members: 40

Description: AmeriCorps Members, a diverse group of young adults, will serve in teams at community agencies in 30 neighborhoods. Activities will include organizing science camps, tutoring/mentoring, coordinating neighborhood crime prevention programs, and serving as youth delinquency prevention counselors.

Contact: Michelle Obama; 312/422-7777; 312/422 -7776 (fax)

IL-13

Decatur:

Program: City of Decatur, Illinois/Decatur AmeriCorps Program

AmeriCorps Members: 20

Description: AmeriCorps Members will serve as youth counselors, crime analysts, domestic violence counselors, recycling specialists, family literacy trainers, and neighborhood outreach specialists in this partnership between the City and sixteen community-based organizations.

Contact: Ms. Carol Fritz; 217/424-2801; 217/424-2770 (fax)

IL-14

Ina:

Program: Rend Lake College/ChildCorps

AmeriCorps Members: 22

Description: AmeriCorps Members, serving as resource specialists and counselors in all 102 Illinois counties, will increase the number of child care providers by recruiting, training and providing technical assistance to prospective and new providers. They will also improve the quality of placements through consumer education.

Contact: Ms. Valarie Dawkins; 618/437-5400; 618/437-5677 (fax)

IL-15

Ina:

Program: Rend Lake College/Americorps in Southern Illinois

AmeriCorps Members:

Description: Planning grant, developed by four post-secondary institutions in southern Illinois, to create a program to engage college students in national service activities to meet the educational needs of at-risk youth. Resulting activities will be family literacy training and counseling of youth.

Contact: Mr. Rex Duncan; 618/437-5321; 618/437-5677 (fax)

IL-16

Springfield:

Program: Illinois Department of Energy and Natural Resources/RiverWatch

AmeriCorps Members: 30

Description: AmeriCorps Members will protect, monitor and restore the state's rivers and streams. Activities will include environmental outreach to community groups, businesses and schools; volunteer recruitment; stream clean-up; habitat evaluation; and biological monitoring.

Contact: Dana Curtiss; 217/785-2800; 217/785-8575 (fax)

IL-17

East St. Louis:

Program: East St. Louis /SIU-Edwardsville AmeriCorps/East St. Louis

Description: AmeriCorps Members will provide tutoring, mentoring, and recreational activities for the children of the Lansdowne community in East St. Louis.

State Priorities:

Education; Environment; Public Safety; Human Needs. Illinois has adopted the

National Priorities, but not the subareas (e.g., "School Readiness").

INDIANA

State Lead Contact:

Amy Conrad Warner
State Student Assistance Commission of
Indiana (SSACI)
150 W. Market St., Suite 500
Indianapolis, IN 46204
Phone: 317/233-4273
Fax: 317/232-3260

1995-96 Programs

National Service Network

IN-1

Statewide:
Program: National Multiple Sclerosis Society/"Bridge to Independence"
AmeriCorps Members: 8 (144 Nationally)
Description: AmeriCorps Members, many of who have Multiple Sclerosis, will work to build awareness about Multiple Sclerosis while coordinating volunteers in extensive living assistance programs—helping disadvantaged people to make it on their own.
Contact: Nancy J. Holland; (212) 476-0453

IN-2

Fort Wayne:
Program: YMCA Earth Service Corps Fellowship
AmeriCorps Members: 40 Nationally
Description: AmeriCorps Members will address local environmental concerns, coordinating park cleanups, urban gardening projects, and environmental symposia.
Contact: Celeste Wroblewski; (312) 269-0506

IN-3

Indianapolis:
Program: Environmental Careers Organization, Inc./Technical Advisor Program for Toxics Use Reduction (TAPTUR)
AmeriCorps Members: 2
Description: AmeriCorps Members will work to protect and enhance the environment

through the development of professionals, the promotion of careers, and the inspiration of individual action.
Contact: Doreen Carey; (219) 473-4246

IN-4

Indianapolis:
Program: YMCA Earth Service Corps Fellowship
AmeriCorps Members: 40 Nationally
Description: AmeriCorps Members will address local environmental concerns, coordinating park cleanups, urban gardening projects, and environmental symposia.
Contact: Celeste Wroblewski; (312) 269-0506

IN-5

Statewide:
Program: YouthBuild USA, Inc./YouthBuild AmeriCorps
Participants 30
Description: AmeriCorps Members will work with community-based organizations to rehabilitate abandoned housing or build new housing for homeless people, people with AIDS, people with disabilities, or very low-income people.
Contact: Bettye Brooks; (219) 944-2930

State and Local

IN-6

Elkhart:
Program: City of Elkhart/Elkhart Enviro-Corps
AmeriCorps Members: 20
Description: AmeriCorps Members will transform a city sludge farm into a nature preserve, restore a polluted swamp to a thriving natural lake, test area drinking water quality, and create environmental public service announcements.
Contact: Mr. Gary Gilot; 219/293-2572; 219/293-7658 (fax)

IN-7

Indianapolis:
Program: Marion County Family Advocacy Center, Inc./Indy Corps
AmeriCorps Members: 20

Description: AmeriCorps Members will help victims of child and spousal abuse access services through a hotline and work in area hospitals, and will also provide alternatives to crime and gang involvement for area youth.
Contact: Ms Cynthia Holmes; 317/327-6916; 317/327-6918 (fax)

IN-8

Indianapolis:
Program: Martin University/Corps of Scholars
AmeriCorps Members: 40
Description: AmeriCorps Members will improve the educational achievement of at-risk youth by tutoring and mentoring high school students and at-risk first year college students, and by tutoring county jail inmates about to be released.
Contact: Dr. Thulani Langa; 317/543-4891

IN-9

Indianapolis:
Program: State Student Assistance Commission of Indiana (SSACI)/21st Century Scholars AmeriCorps Program
AmeriCorps Members: 22
Description: AmeriCorps Members will tutor at-risk students at 9 statewide sites, while SSACI guarantees college aid to students who stay drug, alcohol, and crime free, and maintain a 2.0 grade point average.
Contact: Mr. Philip Seabrook; 317/233-2100; 317/232-3260 (fax)

IN-10

Notre Dame:
Program: University of Notre Dame
AmeriCorps Members: 40
Description: AmeriCorps Members will serve as math, science, and social studies teachers in 30 under-resourced elementary, middle, and high schools throughout the southeastern United States.
Contact: University of Notre Dame

IN-11

Fort Wayne:
Program: Kid's Connection
AmeriCorps Members: 23 part-time
Description: AmeriCorps Members will help to get children involved in programs that have a positive influence on their lives and provide an alternative to violent youth activities.
Contact: Mitch Sheppard; 219/427-6024; 219/427-6020

IN-12

Fortville:
Program: Each One Counts Corps
AmeriCorps Members: 10
Description: AmeriCorps Members will be assigned to a teacher within the school system to provide assistance with the evaluation process and work with elementary students.
Contact: David Heller; 317/485-3180; 317/485-3113 (fax)

IN-13

Indianapolis:
Program: Youth Opportunities for Meeting the Future
AmeriCorps Members: 20
Description: AmeriCorps Members will tutor, conduct exploratory math and science programs, and teach nonviolent behavior skills to youths at 10 neighborhood centers throughout Marion County.
Contact: Dr. Robert Burbacher; 317/639-6106; 317/639-2782

IN-14

Fort Wayne:
Program: LEP (Limited English Proficiency) Volunteer Action Program
AmeriCorps Members: 4 full- and 12 part-time
Description: AmeriCorps Members will assist youth and adults with English proficiency through academic tutoring.
Contact: Jeanne Taylor; 219/425-7329; 219/425-7609 (fax)

IN-15

Jeffersonville:
Program: AmeriCorps Volunteer Department Project

AmeriCorps Members: 10
Description: AmeriCorps Members will improve the health and readiness of 140 children in various counties and will be involved with Head Start programs, child supervision, homeless shelter activities, and parenting skills.
Contact: Beverly Anderson; 812/288-6451; 812/284-8314 (fax)

IN-16

Bloomington:
Program: ARC AmeriCorps
AmeriCorps Members: 5 full- and 10 part-time
Description: AmeriCorps Members will provide support, consultation and training to increase community inclusion for persons with developmental disabilities.
Contact: Leslie Green 812/332-2168; 812/323-4610 (fax)

IN-17

South Bend:
Program: AmeriCorps South Bend
AmeriCorps Members: 10 full- and 3 part-time
Description: AmeriCorps Members will assist the homeless in achieving housing self-sufficiency.
Contact: John Pinter; 219/631-8016; 219/234-0890 (fax)

IN-18

Indianapolis:
Program: AIM AmeriCorps for Indiana Migrants
AmeriCorps Members: 17 part-time
Description: AmeriCorps Members will assist Migrant Head Start Centers to enhance the social competence and health of children of migrant farm workers.
Contact: Jane Tilden; 317/547-1924; 317/547-6597 (fax)

IN-19

Bloomington:
Program: Middle Way House Transitional Housing Program
AmeriCorps Members: 2 full-time and 16 part-time
Description: AmeriCorps Members will help to provide affordable housing and support services to formerly battered women and their children.
Contact: Toby Strout; 812/333-7404; 812/323-9063 (fax)

IN-20

Gary:
Program: YouthBuild Gary
AmeriCorps Members: 30
Description: AmeriCorps Members will rehabilitate abandoned housing and build new housing for homeless persons, persons with AIDS, disabled, and very low income people.
Contact: Twian Peebles; 219/886-7475; 219/885-2246

IN-21

Indianapolis:
Program: 21st Century Scholars AmeriCorps Program
AmeriCorps Members: 27
Description: AmeriCorps Members will provide educational opportunities to 2500 21st Century Scholars.
Contact: Philip A. Seabrook; 317/233-2100; 317/232-3260

IN-22

Indianapolis:
Program: IndyCorps
AmeriCorps Members: 16 full- and 4 part-time
Description: AmeriCorps Members will work to prevent family and youth violence.
Contact: Charlie Wiles; 317/327-6916; 317/327-6918

IN-23

Elkhart:
Program: Elkhart EnviroCorps
AmeriCorps Members: 19
Description: AmeriCorps Members will develop a nature preserve and work on other environmental projects.
Contact: Theresa Campbell; 219/293-2572; 219/293-7658

IN-24

Indianapolis:
Program: YMCA Earth Service Corps
AmeriCorps Members: 5
Description: AmeriCorps Members will

coordinate school based community service clubs that sponsor environmental projects.
Contact: Michelle Goodrich; 317/266-9622; 317/266-2845 (fax)

IN-25

Indianapolis:
Program: Corps of Scholars
AmeriCorps Members: 30 part-time
Description: AmeriCorps Members will tutor and mentor 21st Century Scholars at middle and high schools.
Contact: Dr. Thulani Langa; 317/543-4894; 317/543-3257

IOWA

State Lead Contact:

Barbara J. Finch
Governor's Office on Volunteerism
Office of the Governor
State Capitol
Des Moines, IA 50319
Phone: 515/281-8304
Fax: 515/281-6611

1995-96 Programs

National Service Network

IA-1

Statewide:
Program: Association of Farmworkers Opportunity Programs
AmeriCorps Members: 61 Nationally
Description: AmeriCorps Members will train migrant and seasonal farm workers on how to reduce exposure to pesticides and improve farm workers' access to other health, education, and support services.
Contact: Jim Ramos; 515/244-5694; 515/244-4166 (fax)

IA-2

Statewide:
Program: USDA Rural Development Team
AmeriCorps Members: 78 in the 9 Flood States
Description: Responding to the environmental and economic damage caused by last year's flood, AmeriCorps Members will

assess flood-relief needs, explain wetlands delineation to land owners and work to reduce ground water pollution.
Contact: Jim Ayen; 515/284-4370; 515/284-4394

IA-3

Des Moines:
Program: I Have a Dream Foundation/AmeriCorps Partnership
AmeriCorps Members: 5 (114 Nationally)
Description: Members will mentor and tutor student "Dreamers" from disadvantaged areas, giving personal guidance to prevent dropouts.
Contact: Tomi Johnson; 515/242-7391; 515/242-7360 (fax)

State and Local

IA-4

Ames:
Program: Iowa State University Extension/Iowa College & Community Action Network (ICAN)
AmeriCorps Members: 82
Description: AmeriCorps Members will refurbish 50 elderly owned homes, reduce crime and improve educational attainment by providing after-school tutoring and mentoring, teaching conflict resolution skills, and developing a youth summer leadership session.
Contact: Ms. Wendy Brock; 515/294-1607; 515/294-1047

IA-5

Des Moines:
Program: Iowa Coalition Against Domestic Violence/Domestic Violence Project
AmeriCorps Members: 20
Description: AmeriCorps Members will help victims of domestic violence access social and court services, assist counselors in crisis intervention and peer counseling, and enhance community support systems assisting victims.
Contact: Ms. Sandy Murphy; 515/244-8028; 515/24244-7417 (fax)

IA-6

Marshalltown:
Program: Mid-Iowa Community Action Incorporated/Marshalltown AmeriCorps: Linking Home, School and Community
AmeriCorps Members: 20
Description: AmeriCorps Members will improve low student achievement due to family and poverty related issues by developing 4 school-based Family Development Centers which will link students and families to needed social services and other support agencies.
Contact: Mr. James Swope; 515/752-7162; 515/752-9724 (fax)

IA-7

Des Moines:
Program: AmeriCorps Enterprise Community Service Project
AmeriCorps Members: 4 full- and 32 part-time
Description: Members will work at improving neighborhoods through painting, repairing, cleaning, etc., community policing, and improving academic success of young residents.
Contact: Paula Rees; 515/242-7890; 515/242-7396 (fax)

IA-8

Cedar Rapids:
Program: Neighbors in Action
AmeriCorps Members: 23
Description: Members will work through existing agencies and organizations to establish and support community block watches, recruit families that need social services, and revitalize deteriorating community areas.
Contact: Bill Eckerly; 319/398-3907; 319/398-3684 (fax)

KANSAS

State Lead Contact:

Patricia P. Kells
Kansas Office for Community Service
P.O. Box 889
Topeka, KS 66001

Phone: 913/234-1423
Fax: 913/234-1429

State Commission:

Kansas Commission on National and Community Service

1995-96 Programs

National Service Network

KS-1

Statewide:
(Rural areas)
Program: Association of Farmworkers Opportunity Program
AmeriCorps Members: 1 (61 Nationally)
Description: AmeriCorps Members will train migrant and seasonal farmworkers on how to reduce exposure to pesticides and improve farmworkers access to other health, education and supportive services.
Contact: Sam Demel; 316/264-5372; 316/264-0194

KS-2

Statewide:
Program: USDA Rural Development Team
AmeriCorps Members: 78 in the 9 Flood States
Description: Responding to the environmental and economic damage caused by last year's flood, AmeriCorps Members will assess flood-relief needs, explain wetlands delineation to land owners, and work to reduce ground water pollution.
Contact: Jim Meisenheimer; 913/823-4500; 913/823-4540

KS-3

Program: USDA Public Lands and Environment Team
AmeriCorps Members: 73 in the 9 Flood States
Description: AmeriCorps Members will engage a variety of flood relief work by assessing damage, restoring wetlands, and restoring flood control facilities.
Contact: Jim Meisenheimer; 913/823-4500; 913/823-4540

KS-4

Kansas City:
Program: Kansas City Consensus/Bridges Across the Heartland
AmeriCorps Members: 76
Description: Supported by a coalition of experienced non-profit agencies, Ameri-Corps Members will serve Kansas City urban communities by providing comprehensive response to interrelated community needs.
Contact: Sean Corkrean; 816/753-3398; 816/753-6019 (fax)

KS-5

Shawnee Mission:
Program: National Multiple Sclerosis Society/"Bridge to Independence"
AmeriCorps Members: 8 (144 Nationally)
Description: AmeriCorps Members will work to build awareness about Multiple Sclerosis while coordinating volunteers in extensive living assistance programs—helping disadvantaged people to make it on their own.
Contact: Pat Rittenmaier; 913/432-3926; 913/432-6912 (fax)

State and Local

KS-6

Wichita:
Program: Mennonite Housing Rehabilitation Services, Inc./Mennonite Housing Corps.
AmeriCorps Members: 10
Description: AmeriCorps Members will assist in providing affordable quality housing for low-income, elderly, and disabled home-owners, train volunteers in housing rehabilitation and construction.
Contact: Marlene Turner; 316/942-4848; 316/942-0190 (fax)

KS-7

Hays:
Program: Fort Hays State University/Project SERV
AmeriCorps Members:
Description: AmeriCorps Members will participate in a mentoring program for young people to develop projects to rehabilitate the natural environment, to assist community

agencies in school readiness programs, and to aid criminal justice agencies in crime prevention programs.
Contact: Dee Strong; 913/628-5897; 913/628-4188 (fax)

KS-8

Horton:
Program: Kickapoo Nation/Kickapoo AmeriCorps
AmeriCorps Members: 25
Description: AmeriCorps Members will improve wildlife habitats, provide flood relief, build roads, develop a brush fire containment project, revitalize cultural traditions with elders, and train community members in agriculture and ranching.
Contact: Mr. Steve Stout; 913/474-3403; 913/486-2801 (fax)

KS-9

Kansas City:
Program: United Way of Wyandotte County/United Way Neighborhood Corps of Kansas City, Kansas
AmeriCorps Members: 21
Description: AmeriCorps Members will collaborate with area resident groups to rehabilitate distressed houses, organize art projects, construct playgrounds, create a resident skill bank for service projects, identify 30 new service projects, and recruit resident volunteers.
Contact: Ms. Ann Jurcyk; 913/371-3674; 913/371-2718 (fax)

KS-10

Manhattan:
Program: Kansas State University/Kansas Health and Safety Extension Corps
AmeriCorps Members: 120
Description: AmeriCorps Members will conduct surveys of rural health needs in underserved areas, provide health and safety education for children, develop joint action plans with local organizations to cope with natural disasters, and train adults in CPR, First Aid, and early responder roles in illness.
Contact: Ms. Glendia Henley; 913/532-7721; 913/532-6290 (fax)

KS-11

Topeka:
Program: Topeka Youth Project/Topeka Youth Corps
AmeriCorps Members: 30
Description: AmeriCorps Members will tutor and counsel at-risk primary and middle-school students, assist police substations to reduce crime, administer conflict resolution training, renovate low-income housing, and repair public facilities.
Contact: Dalene Liby; 913/273-4141; 913/273-9417 (fax)

KS-12

Wichita:
Program: Wichita State University/Neighborhood Freedom Corps
AmeriCorps Members: 20
Description: AmeriCorps Members will provide bilingual tutoring for children and adults, assist the DA in a deferred prosecution program, help victims of sexual assault, provide care for disabled individuals, produce a service director for individuals with disabilities, and improve parks.
Contact: Kaye Monk; 316/689-3737; 316/689-3626 (fax)

State Priorities:

Program Development includes:
Strengthening service learning experiences for AmeriCorps members.

KENTUCKY

State Lead Contact:

David Crowley
501 High Street
State Office Bldg.
Room 923
Frankfort, KY 40602
Phone: 502/564-5195
Fax: 502/564-7987

State Commission:

Kentucky Community Service Commission

1995-96 Programs

National Service Network

KY-1

Louisville:
Program: National Center for Family Literacy
AmeriCorps Members: 45
Description: AmeriCorps Members will serve as teachers' assistants in family literacy classrooms and visit homes to tutor family members.
Contact: Robert Spillman; 502/584-1133

KY-2

Louisville:
Program: Summerbridge AmeriCorps Teaching Program
AmeriCorps Members: 68 Nationally
Description: AmeriCorps Members will recruit high school and college students to teach disadvantaged middle school students. The objective will be to improve their academic and leadership performance.
Contact: Delia Decourcy, Adrienne Smith; 502/423-0445

State and Local

KY-3

Frankfort:
Program: Homeless and Housing Coalition of Kentucky, Inc./Getting Things Done for Kentucky's Homeless
AmeriCorps Members: 33
Description: AmeriCorps Members will assist local homeless and low-income families by constructing or rehabilitating 58 affordable housing units, developing six new outreach and service programs, providing care and advocacy services to 500 children of homeless families, and serving 800 families through case management.
Contact: Todd Rogers; 502/223-1834 (phone & fax)

KY-4

Franklin:
Program: Simpson County Board of Education/Service Learning Impacting Children's Education (SLICE)

AmeriCorps Members: 20

Description: AmeriCorps Members will provide individualized mentoring/tutoring and service-learning activities to nearly half the second grade students in this rural county, and will develop a partnership with parents in these efforts.

Contact: Mr. Mike Houston; 502/586-2804; 502/586-2805 (fax)

KY-5

Louisville:

Program: Jefferson County Public Schools/Agencies/Communities Merging Effectively (ACME)

AmeriCorps Members: 22

Description: AmeriCorps Members will, through a four entity collaboration, reduce youth-related crime by providing violence prevention techniques and peer mediation and increasing the academic success of 200 identified youth through community education programs.

Contact: Margaret Ann McCabe; 502/561-0782

KY-6

Morehead:

Program: Morehead State University/MSU-Corps

AmeriCorps Members: 18

Description: AmeriCorps Members will improve the school achievement of high-risk school-age children in eight Appalachian counties by developing and implementing a comprehensive parental involvement, tutoring, and mentoring program.

Contact: Steve Swim; 606/783-2719; 606/783-5026 (fax)

KY-7

Richmond:

Program: Eastern Kentucky University/Student Service Consortium

AmeriCorps Members: 20

Description: AmeriCorps Members will, through a newly established Student Service Consortium, facilitate, coordinate and implement service-learning programs serving kindergarten through post-secondary students statewide. More than 2,500 students will engage in service-learning activities.

Contact: Ms. Nancy Thames; 606/622-6543; 606/622-6526 (fax)

KY-8

Prestonsburg:

Program: AmeriCorps/Appalachian Self-Sufficiency Program

Description: Call contact for information.

Contact: Sue Foltz; 606/886-2374; 606/886-3382 (fax)

KY-9

Hopkinsville:

Program: Hopkinsville Offers People Education (H.O.P.E.)

Description: Call contact for information.

Contact: Sarah Noe Davis; 502/887-1300; 606/887-1316 (fax)

KY-10

Lexington:

Program: Lexington Works

Description: Call contact for information.

Contact: Mark Twitty; 606/244-2257; 606/244-2219 (fax)

KY-11

Florence:

Program: Northern KY Abuse Prevention Corps

Description: Call contact for information.

Contact: Ester Erkins; 606/525-2600; 606/525-1775 (fax)

State Priorities:

The Commission has the responsibility for setting Kentucky Issue Priorities. 8 specific issue priorities have been estimated by the Corporation for National and Community Service, 2 in each of the 4 broad issue areas of education, human needs, public safety and environment. The Commission has adopted 10 issue Priorities. These include the 8 national priorities plus the additional priorities "adult learning" and "community issue based programs" listed below.

EDUCATION

Adult Learning - improving opportunity for adult learning in areas of adult literacy, adult education (e.g., G.E.D. preparation), parenting skills and job skills training.

Community Issue Based - programs that identify and meet local priorities and needs.

LOUISIANA

State Lead Contact:

Sarah Sims
Office of the Lt. Governor
930 North 3rd St.
Baton Rouge, LA 70804
Phone: 504/342-2038
Fax: 504/342-1949

State Commission:

Louisiana Service Commission and Office of Lieutenant Governor

1995-96 Programs

National Service Network

LA-1

Statewide:
Program: Delta Service Corps
AmeriCorps Members: 145 (435 Nationally)
Description: Through a partnership with local community agencies, AmeriCorps Members will assist low-income residents in finding low income housing, tutor children to enhance their literacy skills and work with state parks to conserve and restore the environment.
Contact: Andy Kopplin; 504/379-8500; 504/369-8504 (fax)

LA-2

Program: USDA Rural Development Team
AmeriCorps Members: 67 (Mississippi Delta)
Description: AmeriCorps Members will help communities protect watersheds, improve housing, promote economic development, boost sustainable agriculture and respond to disasters.
Contact: Joel Berg; 202/720-6350

LA-3

New Orleans:
Program: National Institute for Literacy/Literacy AmeriCorps
AmeriCorps Members: 14
Description: Backed by a partnership between Federal agencies and literacy groups, AmeriCorps Members will confront the debilitating literacy problem. In New Orleans, AmeriCorps Members will attack the problem on several fronts while training community members to take over their training duties.
Contact: Michelle Detillier; 504/866-0001

LA-4

New Orleans:
Program: Summerbridge AmeriCorps Teaching Program
AmeriCorps Members: To Be Determined
Description: AmeriCorps Members will recruit high school and college students to teach disadvantaged middle school students. The objective will be to improve their academic and leadership performance.
Contact: Deirdre Johnson; 504/286-2600; Vince Ricci; 504/896-8594

LA-5

Southeastern LA
Program: Teach for America
AmeriCorps Members: 50 (1000 Nationally)
Description: AmeriCorps Members will respond to an acute need for educators and role models in under-served urban and rural areas by innovative teaching methods to the classroom.
Contact: Sarah Newell; 504/381-8163; 504/566-6177 (fax); Andrew Chiapetta 504/566-6187; Suzanne Lynn; 318/425-3411; 318/856-9167 (fax)

LA-6

Southwestern LA
Program: Teach for America
AmeriCorps Members: 35 (1000 Nationally)
Description: AmeriCorps Members will respond to an acute need for educators and role models in under-served urban and rural areas by bringing diverse perspectives on education and introducing innovative teaching methods to the classroom.
Contact: Sarah Newell; 504/381-8163; 504/566-6177 (fax); Andrew Chiapetta 504/566-6187; Suzanne Lynn; 318/425-3411; 318/856-9167 (fax)

LA-7

New Orleans:
Program: Neighborhood Housing
AmeriCorps Members:
Description: AmeriCorps Members will work to improve neighborhoods by addressing housing and safety issues.
Contact: Lauren Anderson; 504/899-5900; 504/899-6190 (fax)

LA-8

Baton Rouge:
Program: Youth Volunteers Corps of america (VolunTEENS)
AmeriCorps Members:
Description: AmeriCorps Members will work with volunteers age 13-18 who wish to improve their community.
Contact: Noel Parnell; 504/927-8270

State and Local

LA-9

Baton Rouge:
Program: Mid City Redevelopment Alliance/SERVE! MID CITY
AmeriCorps Members: 42
Description: AmeriCorps Members will serve the Mid City area by providing crime prevention workshops, helping to repair public housing, helping to rehabilitate facilities, organizing cleanups, working with community health care agencies, administering a "kids-watch" project; reducing truancy; and tutoring children.
Contact: Trudy Bell; 504/346-1000; 504/344-6171 (fax)

LA-10

Lafayette:
Program: University of Southwestern Louisiana/AmeriCorps Scholars of Acadiana
AmeriCorps Members:
Description: University of Southwestern Louisiana will develop a service program to engage student leaders in a co-venture with residents in order to revitalize communities adjacent to the University.
Contact: Grace Depass-Espree; 318/481-5922; 318/482-6195 (fax)

LA-11

Lake Charles:
Program: City of Lake Charles/Volunteers in Police Service
AmeriCorps Members:
Description: The City of Lake Charles will plan to develop a service program in collaboration with the police department in order to improve victim assistance services, assist in the investigations of low-evidence cases, and educate the community about public safety issues.
Contact: Mr. Sam Ivey; 318/491-1317; 318/491-1236 (fax)

LA-12

New Orleans:
Program: New Orleans Youth Action Corps/New Orleans Youth Action Corps
AmeriCorps Members: 70
Description: AmeriCorps members will create an after-school developmental program, establish partnerships with primary and middle schools to administer service-learning projects, create community gardens, renovate distressed housing, and implement environmental projects with residents.
Contact: Ms. Jennifer Cumberbatch; 504/947-6628; 504/947-6066 (fax)

LA-13

Shreveport:
Program: Shreveport Green/ShrevCORPS
AmeriCorps Members: 41
Description: AmeriCorps members will serve Shreveport by developing recycling projects, preventing illegal dumping, reducing vandalism, weatherizing low-income housing, repairing houses for the elderly, and building trails for disabled individuals.
Contact: Ms. Yvonne Lee; 318/222-6455; 318/222-8929 (fax)

LA-14

Leesville
Program: Vernon Community Action Council/Domestic Violence Aid Program
AmeriCorps Members: 6
Description: AmeriCorps Members will provide shelter, support services, education and counseling to female victims of domestic

violence, rape, and sexual assault.
Contact: Tanya Harrell; 318/239-4457; 318/239-0186 (fax)

LA-15

Monroe:
Program: Tri-District Boys and girls Club/Ouchita Parish AmeriCorps
AmeriCorps Members:
Description: AmeriCorps Members will address needs in public housing, control vandalism and juvenile crime rates, develop skills of youth, reduce drug elements, improve literacy, reclaim school dropouts, recover teens from incarceration, and impact poverty and teen health rates.
Contact: Ervin Turner; 318/387-0903; 318/322-0820 (fax)

State Priorities:

The Commission has voted to use the National Priorities for the AmeriCorps grant applications this year. As the Commission holds regional meetings around the State, they are finding that there is good support and agreement with the National Priorities.

MAINE

State Lead Contact:

Robert G. Blakesley
Executive Director, Maine Commission for Community Service
c/o Maine State Planning Office
184 State St., Sta. #38
Augusta, ME 04333
Phone: 207/624-6011
Fax: 207/624-6023

1995-96 Programs

National Service Network

ME-1

Statewide:
(Rural areas)
Program: Association of Farmworkers Opportunity Program

AmeriCorps Members: 2 (61 Nationally)
Description: AmeriCorps Members train migrant and seasonal farmworkers on how to reduce exposure to pesticides and improve farmworkers' access to other health, education and supportive services.
Contact: Jack Frost; 207/945-9431

ME-2

Program: USDA Rural Development Team
AmeriCorps Members: 20
Description: AmeriCorps Members help communities protect watersheds, improve housing, promote economic development, boost sustainable agriculture and respond to disasters.
Contact: Richard Baird; 207/866-7241

ME-3

Portland:
Program: Portland Youth for Public Safety
AmeriCorps Members: 25
Description: AmeriCorps Members are engaged in mediation of community and neighborhood issues, youth conflict resolution, and victim assistance in collaboration with the police department, the public housing authority and other community organizations.
Contact: Lynda Simmons, Director; 207/775-0105

State and Local

ME-4

Augusta:
Program: Workforce Development Centers/College Conservation Corps of Maine
AmeriCorps Members: 20
Description: AmeriCorps Members re-route trails in 4 state parks and 2 cities, stabilize shorelines, clear and mark boundary lines, reconstruct river access points, and operate the Unity Area Recycling Center
Contact: Mr. Kenneth Spalding; 207/287-2068; 207/287-3611 (fax)

State Priorities:

Beginning with National Priorities

MARYLAND

State Lead Contact:

David A. Minges
Governor's Office on Volunteerism
300 West Preston Street
Suite 608
Baltimore, MD 21201
Phone: 410/225-4796
Fax: 410-333-7124
Dr. Marilyn W. Smith
Governor's Commission on Service
Phone: 410/225-1216
Fax: 410/333-7124

1995-96 Programs

National Service Network

MD-1

Statewide:
(Rural areas)
Program: Association of Farmworkers
Opportunity Program
AmeriCorps Members: 1 (61 Nationally)
Description: AmeriCorps Members will
train migrant and seasonal farmworkers on
how to reduce exposure to pesticides and
improve farmworkers' access to other health,
education and support services.
Contact: Lynda Mull; 703/528-4141

MD-2

Baltimore:
Program: Boston University AmeriCorps
Health and Hou. ng Program Fellows
AmeriCorps Members: 10 (31 Nationally)
Description: AmeriCorps Members will
direct a critical health awareness campaign
to stop the spread of HIV and other STD's.
AmeriCorps Members will be recruited from
the Returned Peace Corps Volunteers pro-
gram and will serve while earning their Mas-
ters in Public Health at the Johns Hopkins
University.
Contact: Stella Shiber; 410/955-7540

MD-3

Baltimore:
Program: Department of Transportation
AmeriCorps Members: 20
Description: Together with veteran laborers,

AmeriCorps Members will rehabilitate transportation facilities to make them more acces-
sible for the elderly. In addition members
will be trained in landscaping for urban
green spaces and fixing hazardous sidewalks
for the disabled.
Contact: Cheryl Lockhart;

MD-4

Baltimore/Sandtown
Program: Habitat for Humanity International
AmeriCorps Members: 20
Description: AmeriCorps Members will help
construct 40 housing units in a project that
will involve county-wide officials and community members
Contact: Laverne Cooper; 410/669-3309;
410/523-4781 (fax)

MD-5

Baltimore:
Program: Teach for America
AmeriCorps Members: 90 (1000 Nationally)
Description: Responding to an acute need
for educators and role models in urban and
rural areas, AmeriCorps Members will teach,
advise clubs, and sponsor service activities.
Contact: Roger Schulman; 410/783-1571;
410/783-0138 (fax)

MD-6

Baltimore:
Program: Johns Hopkins School of Nursing/
Health and Housing Fellows
AmeriCorps Members: 10
Description: The Schools of Health at Boston University, the University of Alabama
and the University of Texas, and the School
of Nursing at Johns Hopkins University have
formed the Health and Housing Fellows program to involve Returned Peace Corps Volunteers (RPCVs) in community-based public
health service.
  RPVC AmeriCorps will live and work in
public housing authorities for two calendar
years while studying for a master's degree in
public health at Boston University, the University of Alabama at Birmingham, or the
University of Texas at El Paso; or while
studying for a master's degree in nursing at
Johns Hopkins University. With guidance

from faculty mentors, members will perform a health needs assessment in the community, then design, implement, and evaluate public health intervention in areas such as AIDS and infectious disease, teen pregnancy, violence, and substance abuse prevention. In addition, members will work with housing authority staff on the HUD Family Self Sufficiency Program, a program designed to lessen dependence on public assistance.
Contact: Stella Shiber; 410/955-7540; 410/955-7463 (fax)

MD-7

Baltimore:
Program: Magic Me
AmeriCorps Members: 33 Nationally
Description: AmeriCorps Members will orchestrate self-esteem building and academically motivating service-learning projects directed at adolescents while serving isolated elderly people.
Contact: Drew Carberry; 410/243-9066; 410/243-9076

MD-8

Tacoma Park:
Environmental Careers Organization, Inc./ Technical Advisor Program for Toxics Use Reduction (TAPTUR)
AmeriCorps Members: 1
Description: The Environmental Careers Organization is a national non-profit organization whose mission is to protect and enhance the environment through the development of professionals, the promotion of careers, and the inspiration of individual action. Founded in 1972, its major program has been the Environmental Placement Service, which recruits recent college graduates for environmental internships. In 1993, over 480 associates were placed with federal, state, and local agencies, nonprofit organizations and corporations. The Technical Advisor Program for Toxics Use Reduction (TAPTUR) provides retired engineers and scientists with public service opportunities focused on protecting the environment through pollution prevention.
  TAPTUR AmeriCorps Members will serve communities by researching toxic chemical

substitutes; interpreting technical documents and data; performing non-regulatory facility evaluations to identify reduction opportunities; and assisting citizen groups in developing "Good Neighbor Agreements" with local manufacturing facilities. Members will receive ongoing training on current toxics use reduction methods and technologies.
Contact: Diane Mailey; 617/426-4375

MD-9

Towson:
Program: National Multiple Sclerosis Society/ "Bridge to Independence"
AmeriCorps Members: 8 (144 Nationally)
Description: AmeriCorps Members, many of whom have Multiple Sclerosis, will work to build awareness about Multiple Sclerosis while coordinating volunteers in extensive living assistance programs—helping disadvantaged people to make it on their own.
Contact: Joyce Lehrer; 410/821-8626; 410/821-8030 (fax)

State and Local

MD-10

Annapolis:
Program: Maryland Conservation Corps (MD DNR - Public Lands & Forestry)/ United Youth Corps of Maryland
AmeriCorps Members: 154
Description: AmeriCorps members will meet the needs of rural, urban, and suburban areas of the state through a collaboration between the Maryland Conservation Corps, Civic Works and Community Year. AmeriCorps Members will stabilize erosion, build community gardens and rehabilitate homes for low-income families.
Contact: Laurie Denne; 410/974-3771; 410/974-3158 (fax)

MD-11

Baltimore:
Program: University of Maryland at Baltimore/Enhancing Neighborhood Action By Local Empowerment (ENABLE)
AmeriCorps Members: 23
Description: AmeriCorps Members will conduct home visits of persons with chronic illnesses and provide appropriate referrals for

health services; tutor first grade students; develop structured afterschool intergenerational activities; and teach basic skills to preschool-age children to foster school readiness.

Contact: Dr. Donald Fedder; 410/706-5044; 410/706-0869 (fax)

MD-12

Baltimore:

Program: Neighborhood Reinvestment Corporation/NeighborWorks Community Corps

AmeriCorps Members: 2

Description: The Neighborhood Reinvestment Corporation (NRC) is a 20-year-old public non-profit corporation that provides technical assistance and support to a national network of local partnership organizations. NRC involves neighborhood residents, local businesses (banks, insurance companies, and local merchants) and government agencies. NRC's NeighborWorks Community Corps will introduce AmeriCorps Members to the community development field. Members will improve neighborhoods by bringing people together to address housing and safety issues nationwide. Members will work with local staff in community outreach to increase home ownership, assist with mortgage financing, improve neighborhood appearance, and establish neighborhood watch and safety programs. Members will also work in rehabilitation and construction, recruit volunteers for neighborhood enhancement, and train new home owners in property maintenance.

Contact: Marcella Williams; 202/376-3216; 202/376-3213

MD-13

Baltimore:

Program: Action for the Homeless, Inc./ HOME CORPS

AmeriCorps Members: 22

Description: AmeriCorps Members will help homeless individuals locate and sustain permanent housing, access community resources to maintain self-sufficiency, assist 1575 households in preventing homelessness, secure additional resources and initiate volunteer recruitment, all to reduce home-

lessness in Maryland.

Contact: Al Brown; 410/659-0300; 410/659-0996 (fax)

MD-14

Bowie:

Program: Bowie State University/Maryland Students Taking Responsibility for Tomorrow - MSTART

AmeriCorps Members: 35

Description: AmeriCorps Members will academically strengthen low-income students in a tri-county area using a cascading leadership model by tutoring and supervising high school students who, in turn, act as mentors and tutors for middle and elementary school students.

Contact: Michael Dunn; 301/464-7862; 301/464-7786 (fax)

MD-15

Crownsville:

Program: Governor's Office on Volunteerism/Volunteer Maryland!

AmeriCorps Members: 124

Program: AmeriCorps Members will develop volunteer programs in community-based organizations and public agencies to address Maryland's most pressing needs. Service projects will include building houses in partnership with Habitat for Humanity, organizing service activities for school-aged children and helping low-income women start their own businesses.

Contact: Cathy Brill; 410/514-7270; 410/514-7277 (fax)

MD-16

Frostburg:

Program: Frostburg State University/A STAR! IN WESTERN MARYLAND Appalachian Service through Action and Resources

AmeriCorps Members: 25

Description: AmeriCorps members will provide independent living assistance, enlarge area food pantries, create youth literacy programs, and develop educational programs for Head Start students in Appalachian Maryland.

Contact: Linda Dahlen; 301/687-7599; 301/689-7049 (fax)

MD-17

Silver Spring:
Program: Montgomery County Government
Department of Police/AMERICORPS
MARYLAND-COMMUNITY ASSISTING
POLICE
AmeriCorps Members: 30
Description: AmeriCorps members will
work as victim assistance advocates, reaching crime victims and complainants to identify problems and access resources; as
community mobilizers to prevent public
safety problems; and as crime prevention
trainers for 1000 senior citizens.
Contact: Phil Andrews; 301/565-7575; 301/
565-5860 (fax)

MASSACHUSETTS

State Lead Contact:

Bradford J. Minnick
Deputy Chief Secretary
Office of the Governor
State House; Room 259
Boston, MA 02133
Phone: 617/727-5787
Fax: 617/727-8136

Additional Contact:

Melora Balson
Massachusetts Community Service
Commission
c/o Massachusetts Youth Service Alliance
87 Summer St. 4th Floor
Boston, MA 02210
Phone: 617/542-2544
Fax: 617/542-0240

1995-96 Programs

National Service Network

MA-1

Becket:
Program: YMCA Earth Service Corps Fellowship
AmeriCorps Members: 40 Nationally
Description: AmeriCorps Members will
address local environmental concerns, coordinating park cleanups, urban gardening

projects, and environmental symposia.
Contact: Elsa Bengel; 617/536-7800; 617/
536-3240 (fax)

MA-2

Boston:
Program: Boston University AmeriCorps
Health and Housing Program Fellows
AmeriCorps Members: 10
Description: AmeriCorps Members will
direct a critical health awareness campaign
to stop the spread of HIV and other STD's.
AmeriCorps Members will be recruited from
the Returned Peace Corps Volunteers program and will serve while earning their Mas-
ters in Public Health at Boston University.
Contact: Elizabeth Ollen; 617/638-4290;
617/638-5299 (fax)

MA-3

Boston:
Program: Green Corps' Neighborhood
Green Corps Program
AmeriCorps Members: 60 Nationally
Description: Splitting their time between
projects involving the home environment
and the community environment, Ameri-
Corps Members will educate and then activate their communities through three
projects: low income home weatherization,
lead paint abatement, and urban gardening.
Contact: Ms. Leslie Samuelrich; 617/426-
8506; 617/292-8057

MA-4

Boston:
Program: USDA Public Lands and Environment Team
AmeriCorps Members: 20
Description: Replacing inner-city environmental hazards with recreation areas and
green spaces, AmeriCorps volunteers will
combat urban neglect and teach the inner-
city population about the project in several
languages.
Contact: Mark MacQueen; 508/295-1481;
508/291-2368 (fax)

MA-5

Boston:
Program: YMCA Earth Service Corps Fellowship

AmeriCorps Members: 40 Nationally
Description: AmeriCorps Members will address local environmental concerns, coordinating park cleanups, urban gardening projects, and environmental symposia.
Contact: Elsa Bengel; 617/536-7800; 617/536-3240 (fax)

MA-6

Brockton:
Program: YMCA Earth Service Corps Fellowship
AmeriCorps Members: 40 Nationally
Description: AmeriCorps Members will address local environmental concerns, coordinating park cleanups, urban gardening projects, and environmental symposia.
Contact: John Bengel; 508/584-1100, ext. 18

MA-7

Cambridge:
Program: Summerbridge AmeriCorps Teaching Program
AmeriCorps Members: 68 Nationally
Description: AmeriCorps Members will recruit high school and college students to teach disadvantaged middle school students. The objective will be to improve their academic and leadership performance.
Contact: Sarah Feldman; 617/349-6400; 617/349-6515 (fax)

MA-8

Fall River:
Program: YMCA Earth Service Corps Fellowship
AmeriCorps Members: 40 Nationally
Description: AmeriCorps Members will address local environmental concerns, coordinating park cleanups, urban gardening projects, and environmental symposia.
Contact: Carol Measom; 508/675-7841; 508/675-0250 (fax)

MA-9

Springfield:
Program: National Service Legal Corps
AmeriCorps Members:
Description: Working with domestic violence programs throughout Western Massachusetts, AmeriCorps Members will assist battered women in resolving civil legal prob-

lems and obtaining freedom from the batterer.
Contact: Andrew Steinberg; 413/781-7814; 413/746-3221

MA-10

Waltham:
Program: National Multiple Sclerosis Society/ "Bridge to Independence"
AmeriCorps Members: 8 (144 Nationally)
Description: AmeriCorps Members, many of whom have Multiple Sclerosis, will work to build awareness about Multiple Sclerosis while coordinating volunteers in extensive living assistance programs—helping disadvantaged people to make it on their own.
Contact: Susan Fliegel; 617/890-4990; 617/890-2089 (fax)

State and Local

MA-11

Boston:
Program: City Year Boston/City Year: A Beacon for the Nation
AmeriCorps Members: 330
Description: AmeriCorps Members in this diverse Corps will tutor and mentor urban children in 15 urban public schools, day care of Head Start Centers; transform vacant lots into community gardens; design and conduct violence prevention and HIV/AIDS awareness workshops for children and teenagers; and rehabilitate affordable housing.
Contact: Meredith Weenick; 617/350-0728; 617/350-0562 (fax)

MA-12

Boston/Cambridge:
Program: Local Initiative Support Corporation
AmeriCorps Members:
Description: AmeriCorps Members will work assisting local community revitalization efforts. Specific areas include housing outreach and education, community policing, job training, youth education programs, affordable housing financing and development and neighborhood planning.
Contact: Robyn Roman; 617/338-0412; 617/338-2209 (fax)

MA-13

Boston:
Program: Magic Me/Boston
AmeriCorps Members: 5
Description: AmeriCorps Members will orchestrate self-esteem building and academically motivating service-learning projects directed at adolescents while serving isolated elderly people.
Contact: Sherry Ziplow; 617/354-2100; 617/354-2182

MA-14

Brockton:
Program: Old Colony Y Services Corps/ CITY PRIDE, Brockton's Urban Youth Serve Corps
AmeriCorps Members: 24
Description: AmeriCorps Members will initiate citywide curbside recycling, repair athletic equipment in neighborhood parks, paint the exterior of a housing development and clean up and beautify the area surrounding the development.
Contact: Mr. John Bengel; 508/584-1100 ext 18; 508/427-4369 (fax)

MA-15

Cambridge:
Program: Cambridge Community Services/ Academic for Changing Times (A.C.T.)
AmeriCorps Members: 20
Description: AmeriCorps members will provide intensive after-school educational services to middle school-aged youth, adolescents who are making the transition to high school, and new immigrant high school youth adjusting to American culture and educational practices.
Contact: Virginia Gold; 617/876-5214; 617/876-8187 (fax)

MA-16

Lawrence:
Program: Lawrence Youth Commission/ Lawrence Youth Commission City CORE
AmeriCorps Members: 30
Description: AmeriCorps Members will work in middle schools as teacher's aids; build homes for low-income and elderly residents; remove illegal dumping in natural neighborhood environments; and establish a food-sharing program for low-income and elderly residents.
Contact: Mr. Andrew Mente; 508/681-0548; 508/794-2552 (fax)

MA-17

Lowell:
Program: Lowell YMCA/Neighborhood Service Corp
AmeriCorps Members: 10
Description: AmeriCorps Members will tutor and mentor school-age youth; assist in early intervention programs at day care centers and Head Start programs; and implement anti-violence projects in cooperation with the new Police Department substation.
Contact: Mike Chadwick; 508/458-9983; 508/458-4451

MA-18

Pittsfield:
Program: Berkshire Training and Employment Program/Berkshire Conservation Team
AmeriCorps Members: 11
Description: AmeriCorps Members will cut, stack, and clear trees in a state park; perform mosquito control techniques; and design and implement an educational curriculum for 7th graders. This program offers non-traditional career opportunities to young women while addressing the environmental needs of Berkshire County.
Contact: Dennis DeSantis; 413/499-2220; 413/499-0503 (fax)

MA-19

Revere:
Program: ROCA Inc. of North Suffolk Mental Health Association/Youth STAR (Service Taking Action in Revere)
AmeriCorps Members: 20
Description: AmeriCorps Members of diverse ethnic backgrounds will operate a tuberculosis prevention and control project, an HIV prevention project, a food pantry project for poor families, and an emergency response project to deal with floods, fires and blizzards. This is the only corps in the country founded by Cambodian youth.
Contact: Molly Baldwin; 617/889-5210; 617/889-2145 (fax)

MA-20

Roxbury:
Program: YouthBuild Boston, Inc./Youth-Build Boston
AmeriCorps Members: 94
Description: AmeriCorps Members will conduct toxic site investigation on vacant lots slated for development; renovate abandoned property into affordable housing for low-income families; and develop and implement a violence and dropout prevention program in area schools.
Contact: Anita Burke-Johnson; 617/445-8887; 617/427-3950 (fax)

MA-21

Springfield:
Program: Corporation for Public Management/Linking Lifetime AmeriCorps
AmeriCorps Members: 15
Description: AmeriCorps Members will enable youth involved with crime or at risk of becoming involved with crime to pursue positive alternatives. This intergenerational team will tutor, provide life skills training, and implement substance abuse and AIDS awareness education programs.
Contact: Jack Petropolous; 413/737-8911; 413/731-5399 (fax)

MA-22

Worcester:
Program: Worcester Community Action Council/CITYWORKS
AmeriCorps Members: 30
Description: AmeriCorps Members will present a violence prevention/conflict resolution program for middle school students; prevent arson by introducing the "Learn not to Burn" program; and survey elderly clients to design and present an educational nutrition program.
Contact: Robin Allard; 508/754-1176; 508/754-0203 (fax)

MA-23

Becket:
Program: Becket Chimney Corners YMCA
Description: Call contact for information
Contact: Becky Barton; 413/623-8991; 413/623-5890 (fax)

MA-24

Holyoke:
Program: Greater Holyoke Foundation, Inc.
Description: Call contact for information
Contact: Ann McFarland Burke; 413/536-4611; 538-9716 (fax)

MA-25

Roxbury:
Program: National Alliance of VESO
Description: Call contact for information
Contact: Ralph Cooper; 617/445-7030; 617/445-9285 (fax)

MA-26

Northfield:
Program: National Council of Educational Opportunities Association
Description: Call contact for information
Contact: Tom Putnam; 413/498-3416; 413/498-3154 (fax)

MA-27

Boston:
Program: Northeastern University
Description: Call contact for information
Contact: Susan Leitao; 617/373-4025; 413/373-4566 (fax)

MA-28

South Boston:
Program: Notre Dame Mission Volunteer Program
Description: Call contact for information
Contact: Sister Maria Delaney; 617/268-1912; 617/268-3540 (fax)

MA-29

Boston:
Program: Parents United for Childcare
Description: Call contact for information
Contact: Susan DiGiammarino; 617/426-8288; 617/542-1515 (fax)

MA-30

Boston:
Program: UMass Boston
Description: Call contact for information
Contact: Francis Caro; 617/87-7327; 617/287-7080 (fax)

MA-31

Somerville:
Program: US Catholic Conference
Description: Call contact for information

Contact: Claire Carroll; 617/625-1920; 617/629-2246 (fax)

MICHIGAN

State Lead Contact:

Frank Dirks, Executive Director
Michigan Community Service Commission
111 S. Capitol Ave.
Olds Plaza Building
Lansing, MI 48909
Phone: 517/335-4295
Fax: 517/373-4977

State Commission:

Michigan Community Service Commission

1995-96 Programs

National Service Network

MI-1

Statewide:
Program: USDA Rural Development Teach
AmeriCorps Members: 20 (Great Lakes)
Description: AmeriCorps Members will help communities protect watersheds, improve housing, promote economic development, boost sustainable agriculture and respond to disasters.
Contact: Joel Berg; 202/720-6350

MI-2

Detroit:
Program: Youth Volunteer Corps of America/YVCA Leadership Corps
AmeriCorps Members: 10 (107 Nationally)
Description: AmeriCorps Members will develop, run, and enroll volunteers in service projects including: summer camps, academic enrichment programs, service-learning curricula, conflict resolution training, gang alternative programs, and identification of high crime areas.
Contact: David Battey; 913/432-9822

MI-3

Southfield:
Program: National Multiple Sclerosis Society/"Bridge to Independence"
AmeriCorps Members: 8 (144 Nationally)

Description: AmeriCorps Members, many of whom have Multiple Sclerosis, will work to build awareness about Multiple Sclerosis while coordinating volunteers in extensive living assistance programs—helping disadvantaged people to make it on their own.
Contact: Rose Taylor; 810/350-0020; 810/350-0029 (fax)

MI-4

Southwest Michigan:
Program: Youth Volunteer Corps of America/YVCA Leadership Corps
AmeriCorps Members: 7 (107 Nationally)
Description: AmeriCorps Members will develop, run, and enroll volunteers in service projects including: summer camps, academic enrichment programs, service-learning curricula, conflict resolution training, gang alternative programs, and identification of high crime areas.
Contact: David Battey; 913/432-9822

State and Local

MI-5

Ann Arbor:
Program: The Regents of The University of Michigan/The Michigan AmeriCorps Community Service Plan
AmeriCorps Members: 40
Description: AmeriCorps Members will serve pre-schoolers, plan neighborhood watch programs, involve residents in health programs, clean vacant lots, and coordinate crime prevention seminars and housing rehabilitation. This program is a partnership between U of M and community organizations in Detroit.
Contact: Mr. Edwin Miller; 313/764-1408

MI-6

East Lansing
Program: Michigan State University/Environmental Problem Solving in Lansing, Michigan
AmeriCorps Members: 40
Description: AmeriCorps Members will join neighborhood residents to plan, implement and evaluate community environmental projects. Activities will include landscaping vacant lots, restoring wetlands, starting com-

munity food gardens, monitoring noise and air pollution, assessing soil erosion, planting in urban areas.

Contact: Mr. Frank Fear; 517/355-3421; 517/353-8994 (fax)

MI-7

Flint:
Program: United Way of Genesee and Lapeer Counties/Genesee County AmeriCorps Program (GCAP)
AmeriCorps Members: 25
Description: AmeriCorps Members will reduce the number of children exposed to lead-based paint, increase recycling efforts, ensure access to preventive health services, assist in housing rehabilitation, and develop neighborhood safe havens for at-risk youth.
Contact: Mr. Melvyn Brannon; 810/789-7611; 810/787-4518 (fax)

MI-8

Grand Rapids:
Program: Grand Rapids Service Corps/ Grand Rapids Service Corps
AmeriCorps Members: 33
Description: AmeriCorps Members will, in teams, expand the Homework Club, develop an after-school recreation program at a community center, assist in the development of an immunization program for pre-school students, and organize neighborhood clean-ups and cultural activities for children.
Contact: Ms. Mary Moomaw; 616/771-0358; 616/771-0329 (fax)

MI-9

Rochester:
Program: Oakland University/AmeriCorps Oakland
AmeriCorps Members: 40
Description: AmeriCorps Members, in teams coordinated with Pontiac schools, Oakland Probate Court and community organizations, will enable at-risk youth, including those on probation, to re-enter school and the community. Activities include tutoring, mentoring, and revitalizing city parks and community gardens.
Contact: Ms. Joyce Esterberg; 810/370-3213; 810/370-3254 (fax)

MI-10

Saginaw:
Program: United Way of Saginaw County/ Saginaw AmeriCorps
AmeriCorps Members: 40
Description: AmeriCorps Members will work with the Police Department on community policing efforts, serve as youth employment counselors, tutor and mentor in schools, conduct outreach to at-risk youth, be involved in gang prevention activities and develop child care placements.
Contact: P. Laine Blasch; 517/755-0505; 517/755-2158 (fax)

MI-11

Shelby:
Program: American Youth Foundation/ Rural Strategic Action Initiative
AmeriCorps Members:
Description: Planning grant developed by the American Youth Foundation in collaboration with the Department of Social Services and Community Mental Health Services, to create a "rural strategic action initiative" in three western rural counties to prevent family breakdown by developing prevention and support services.
Contact: Mr. Bruce Bailey; 616/861-2262; 616/861-5244 (fax)

MI-12

Southfield:
Program: Big Brothers Big Sisters of Metropolitan Detroit/CircleNet
AmeriCorps Members: 20
Description: AmeriCorps Members will build a "CircleNet" of friends, including Big Brothers/Sisters, for 100 developmentally disabled youth. Activities in the CircleNet include tutoring, mentoring, counseling and assisting with locating employment and apartments.
Contact: Mr. Joseph Radelet; 810/569-0626; 810/569-7322 (fax)

MI-13

Ypsilanti:
Program: Eastern Michigan University/ AmeriCorps: Teams for School Success
AmeriCorps Members: 32